D1503360

THE POLICE IN AMERICAN SOCIETY

THE POLICE IN AMERICAN SOCIETY

Edward F. Dolan and Margaret M. Scariano

1988
Franklin Watts
New York   London   Toronto   Sydney

Photographs courtesy of: Magnum Photos, Inc.: pp. 16 (Burt Glinn), 49 (Leonard Freed), 52 (Ferdinando Schianna), 86 and 107 (Leonard Freed); Photo Researchers, Inc.: pp. 20 (Spencer Grant), 23 (Eugene Gordon), 104 (Fred Lombardi), 153 (Spencer Grant); AP/ Wide World Photos: pp. 26, 66, 118; FBI: pp. 42, 53; ROTHCO Cartoons: pp. 96 (Pierotti); 100 (Renault/Sacramento Bee, Cal.), 111 (A. Ross); Fairfax County Police Department: pp. 121, 140; Newsweek Photo: p. 126 (Bernard Gotfryd); Nancy Hawkins: pp. 128, 132.

Library of Congress Cataloging-in-Publication Data

Dolan, Edward F., 1924–
The police in American society / Edward F. Dolan and Margaret
M. Scariano.
p.   cm.
Bibliography: p.
Includes index.
Summary: Examines the widely varying duties of law enforcement officials and how their functions affect society, discussing the impact of their presence and their role in maintaining order and keeping the peace.
ISBN 0-531-10608-X
1. Police—Juvenile literature.   2. Police—United States—
Juvenile literature.   3. Public relations—United States—Police—
Juvenile literature.   4. Police—United States—Complaints
against—Juvenile literature.   5. Police social work—United
States—Juvenile literature.   [1. Police.]   I. Scariano,
Margaret.   II. Title.
HV7922.D65   1988
363.2'0973—dc19   88-14265   CIP   AC

Contents

THE POLICE IN
AMERICAN SOCIETY

Acknowledgments

We are indebted to many people for their help in the preparation of this book. In particular, for their fine comments and helpful advice during the writing of our manuscript, our gratitude must go to Maurice Lafferty, associate professor of criminal justice, College of Marin, Kentfield, California; Kevin Mullen, Deputy Chief of Police (retired), San Francisco Police Department; and Roy Lotz, associate professor of sociology, John Jay School of Criminal Justice. For special information, our thanks to William R. Royse, formerly of the California Department of Corrections; and six West Coast police officers, all of whom asked not to be identified.

For providing us with needed research materials, may we express our appreciation to the offices of Mayor Robert L. Flynn and Police Commissioner Francis M. Roache, Boston; Chief of Police Daryl F. Gates, Los Angeles; Chief of Police Joseph D. McNamara, San Jose, California; Chief of Police Frank Jordan, San Francisco; and the Police Commission of the City and County of San Francisco, Dr. David Sanchez, Jr., President.

For answering specifics of our questions, our gratitude goes to the offices of public information and media relations of the Chicago Police Department, the Miami Police Department, the New York City Police Department, the San Jose Police Department, and the Washington, D.C. Police Department.

Introduction
The Police in the United States

This book is about the men and women who make up our nation's municipal police forces. They play an all-important role in United States society. Without them, our cities, towns, and villages would be without a system for preserving the civilized way of doing things that is necessary for the survival of a community. There would be no system for maintaining the public order and enforcing the laws by which we live. We would live in chaos.

But the way in which many municipal police officers play their role has long been the target of widespread public complaint and criticism. They have been accused of failing to stem the crime and violence that so mar life in the United States today. They have been accused of harassing and bullying members of the public and of treating suspects with outright brutality. They have been accused of corrupt acts ranging from being "on the take" (accepting money to protect local gamblers and the like) to participating in and profiting from crimes.

In all, the picture of how the municipal police are playing their role in U.S. society is a confusing one. How many officers are good and dedicated workers? How many are "bad apples"? How well or how poorly are the police meeting their responsibilities to maintain the public order, enforce the law, and fight crime?

The purpose of this book is to try to answer these and myriad other questions concerning our municipal police. It is hoped that in so doing we will come to a better understanding of police work itself, of its successes and failures, of the justice or injustice in the public complaints, and of what the police are doing to meet those complaints. And, by speaking of the complaints leveled against the police today, it is hoped that we will reach a better understanding of how Americans everywhere would like their police to perform in the future.

This understanding is of vital importance to anyone who desires to be a responsible citizen and who wants the police to be as responsible as he or she.

One point must be made immediately. There are three levels of law enforcement in the United States—the federal, state, and local. The municipal police belong to the local level. They—and no other level of law enforcement—are to be the subjects of this book. However, in speaking of their problems, we will in a sense be speaking of the problems of all law enforcement agencies because similar problems are found at every level of policing.

For your general information, however, you should know that law enforcement at the federal level is carried out by eight agencies: the Federal Bureau of Investigation; the Drug Enforcement Administration; the Immigration Border Patrol; the U.S. Customs Service; the U.S. Secret Service; the Bureau of Alcohol, Tobacco, and Firearms; the Postal Inspection Service; and the U.S. Coast Guard.

The agencies at the state level vary in number from state to state. The number and type found in any state depend on the needs of that state. State forces are usually called by such names as the state police, highway patrol, and state patrol.

At the local level, the two main agencies are the municipal police department and the county sheriff's department. The municipal department serves the incorporated areas (the towns and cities) in a county, while the sheriff's department serves the people living outside the incorporated areas. In locales where the boundaries of a city and county are exactly the same, the sheriff is usually responsible for such duties as maintaining jail facilities.

By far the greatest number of police officers work for the municipal departments, also known as city or metropolitan departments. And so, of all the law enforcement agencies in the nation, the one with which we most often deal in the course of our lives is the municipal department. Both night and day, we encounter municipal officers whenever we run into trouble—from the very minor to the very serious—within the limits of a city, town, or village.

Now let's see how these officers are doing as they play out their role in society and meet the numerous public complaints and criticisms directed against them.

The local precinct is a hub of activity.

The Police Officer
The Job and an Angry Public

Let's start by pretending that you are a police officer in one of our nation's cities, towns, or villages. You belong to what is known as a municipal police department, and whether you are a policeman or policewoman, you play a very definite role in our society. It is a role that can be simply stated. You hold and exercise the authority to maintain the public order and enforce the laws under which your community lives.

Your role is shared by officers in municipal departments all across the world. It is one that has been needed ever since the time, eons ago, when human beings first gathered together in communities and began to experience all the problems—from accidents and squabbles to criminal acts—that have always gone hand in hand with close living conditions. Someone had to be available to help solve those problems and make life safer. The police officer was, and still is, that someone.

Though your role can be simply stated, those problems have always made the actual task of maintaining the public

17

order and enforcing the law a highly complex one. That task demands that you perform many different and varied duties. Difficult enough in itself, it is also a job that has been made more difficult by the angry criticisms of vast segments of the public. The criticisms date back centuries and are heard in all parts of the world. They are directed at the way in which many police officers fail in their duty or abuse the authority that society has placed in their hands.

Here in the United States, the criticisms have pointed up two sharply contrasting public ideas about the police. Many people feel that, in maintaining law and order, some officers overuse their authority and are guilty of such wrongs as mistreating suspected or arrested persons. On the other hand, just as many people believe that the police have not acted firmly enough in preserving law and order and have failed at their job of fighting crime.

We will see the first of these criticisms within a few pages. But, first, to understand fully the police officer's— that is, your—role in our society, we need to look at those many and varied duties that you perform as you work to maintain the public order and enforce the law.[1]

MAINTAINING THE PUBLIC ORDER

Let's start by watching you encounter a number of situations while patrolling your assigned area—your "beat." You must attend to them all in the name of maintaining the public order:

> On passing a shopping center, you glimpse a five-year-old boy crying in the parking lot. You stop, comfort him, and learn that he has wandered away from his mother. Then you take him by the hand and tour the center until you find his mother.

> Late at night, neighbors on your beat call headquarters to complain that a husband and wife are

*staging a noisy argument out on their front lawn.
Word of the trouble reaches you via your car radio.
You hurry to the scene and put an end to the squabble by calming the couple.*

*Again at night, you sight the back door of a store
standing ajar as you drive down an alley. For safety's sake, you immediately summon another patrol
car to act as your backup. Once the car has arrived,
you enter the store to see if it is being burglarized
or if the owner has merely forgotten to close the
door. Finding no one inside, you have your headquarters notify the owner so that he or she can
investigate the premises to make certain that nothing is missing—and to make certain that he or she
remembers to lock the door in the future as a precaution against possible thefts.*

*You're sent to an intersection where two cars have
collided. You check for injuries, give first aid and
call for an ambulance if necessary, take reports from
the drivers and witnesses on how the accident occurred, and direct traffic around the accident site.*

These are just four of the myriad jobs you may be called
on to do at any time. A great many more are equally familiar
to you and your fellow officers everywhere. For example,
a holiday parade is held; you're on duty to see that the
spectators enjoy the festivities in peace and safety. A distraught teenager, intent on suicide, appears on the roof of
a building and threatens to jump; you call for the fire department to bring safety nets, summon medical help, then
climb to the roof and try to talk the youngster into a change
of mind. An elderly man falls facedown on the sidewalk;
you investigate to see if he is sick, injured, or unconscious
from too much drink; then you take whatever action is
necessary, calling for an ambulance if medical attention is
needed or a patrol wagon if the man is intoxicated and
must be placed in custody until he has recovered.

A police officer takes notes on witnesses' accounts of an auto accident.

The term "maintaining the public order" strikes some police officials as an inadequate one. Why? Because, in the minds of many people, it conjures up just one picture— the picture of you standing on a street corner or cruising the block in a squad car and, by your very presence, discouraging anyone from getting into trouble. This, indeed, is part of your job. But, as the above examples make clear, your duties are far broader. They call for you to handle and solve any problem—from the most minor to the most serious—that disrupts or threatens to disrupt the peace of the community or any of its members. For this reason, the task of "maintaining the public order" might be better described as "keeping the public peace."

ENFORCING THE LAW

Now, what of your law enforcement duties? They usually overlap with your peace-keeping work because the breaking of a law often involves a violation of the public peace. In a very commonplace example, an automobile roars

20

through town at a speed dangerous to everyone on the street. You give chase and stop the car, in part to safeguard the public peace by ending the threat of an accident, in part to apprehend the driver for wantonly ignoring the speed laws or driving while intoxicated.

The same holds true when you're called upon to keep a beggar from stopping people on the sidewalk. You're restoring quiet for the passersby while also enforcing the laws against public nuisances and disturbing the peace.

The same can also be said for very serious crimes. A burglary, an armed robbery, a rape, a gang attack on a citizen, a murder—all are crimes that can violate the peace of a neighborhood or an entire city. When you come face-to-face with a serious crime, what role do you play? To see, again let's pretend that we're watching you at work.

Your car radio crackles. A nearby jewelry store has just been robbed. The robber has fled and disappeared. You make your way to the store, calm everyone, ascertain what has been taken, and begin to ask a series of questions of the witnesses: What happened to each of them? Can they describe the robber? Was the robber a man or a woman? If a man, how tall was he? What was his approximate weight? His age? The color of his hair? His eyes? His skin? You make notes of all that you hear and see. Later, your notes will go into a written report meant to assist the future investigation of the robbery. If you're working in a small town with a force of just a few officers, you may handle that investigation yourself. If you're with a big-city department, the matter will usually be turned over to the department's detectives, whose job it is to conduct criminal investigations. You may be called upon to assist them.

Again, your car radio crackles. This time, a robbery is reported as being in progress. Your job now is to

*arrive at the scene before the robber departs and,
if possible, apprehend him or her. Even if the robber
is caught red-handed, the witnesses to the crime
will have to be questioned for the report that will
be needed to help take the case to trial. You will
likely be summoned to testify at the trial.*

*You're called to a hotel room where the body of a
murder victim has been found. One of your prime
duties here is to protect the site so that evidence
(such as possibly incriminating fingerprints on the
furniture) can be discovered and photographs can
be taken of the room exactly as it was at the time
of the killing. You make certain that no one moves
or even touches anything. Though there are no witnesses, you question people in the hotel—and in
the surrounding neighborhood—for information
that might eventually help to solve the crime.*

As is true of your peace-keeping duties, many other
law enforcement jobs may come your way. You may spend
long hours keeping a suspected criminal under surveil-
lance. Or you may be sent to investigate a gang fight that
has ended with a youth dead or critically injured. On top
of all else, you'll be expected to watch your beat closely
and take whatever steps are possible to prevent crimes from
being committed there.

A NEW POLICE ROLE

In recent years, your peace-keeping and law enforcement
responsibilities have been joined by a new role.[2]

This new role stems from the fact that the United States
today is served by numerous local public and private agencies meant to help people in difficulty. A few agencies of
this sort have been in existence for many years (for ex-

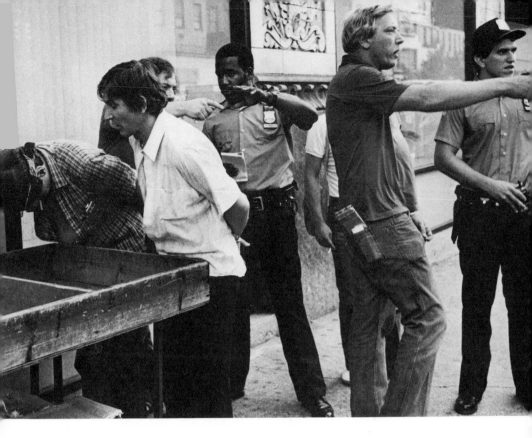

Uniformed and plainclothes police officers with two men arrested for driving while intoxicated

ample, the nation's first child-protection agency, the New York Society for the Prevention of Cruelty to Children, dates back to the 1870s). But the number has increased greatly—and the types of service rendered have grown more varied—ever since the 1960s, an era that, for various reasons, witnessed a great jump in the public's concern for the plight of troubled people. Today, within reach of virtually every American, agencies are standing ready to help people with such diverse problems as alcohol and drug abuse, child and spouse abuse, mental and emotional disorders, homelessness, rape, attempted suicide, and juvenile misbehavior.

23

Because of the presence of these many agencies, your role as a police officer now carries an additional duty. It can be called your "referral duty."

To see how this new responsibility works, let's look again at the family squabble mentioned at the start of the chapter. Let's say that, as you arrive on the scene, the husband lashes out at the wife with his fist, strikes her in the face, and knocks her to the ground. In times past, after stepping between the two and restoring peace, you might have settled things by suggesting that the husband spend the rest of the night at a hotel. Or you might have had the wife go to the home of a friend or relative. You'd have taken either step to give the couple time to cool their tempers before resuming their life together.

Today, you work differently. In your area, there is an agency to which battered wives can go for help. You're able to contact the agency immediately and place her in its care. The agency locates accommodations for the night or for as long as the woman needs them. The agency not only finds the accommodations but also sees that any injuries she may have sustained receive medical care.

Now suppose the wife tells you that tonight's squabble is but the latest of many and that the husband has constantly beaten her over the past months or years. These facts, which will be contained in your report of the matter, may lead the authorities to arrest the husband or order him to be counseled by an agency. The authorities may also decide to have the woman and the husband attend counseling sessions together in an effort to solve their problem.

Your referral duty works in many other cases. Remember the man who collapsed on the street? Suppose you know him to be a longtime alcoholic. There was a time when you might have taken any of three steps—jailed him for the night in a "drunk tank," sent him to a hospital for a few hours to "dry out," or, if you knew him well, even driven him home. Today, you're in a position to do more—to refer him to an agency or a hospital program meant to

24

help him overcome his problem through medical treatment and counseling.

In many instances, you refer troubled people to the agencies because the agencies are there to help and because you know that their personnel are well equipped to handle specific problems. But, in certain other instances—cases of child and spouse abuse, for example—the law *requires* that agency help be sought.

Many police officials say that your referral duty, as new as it is, has become so important that it has joined your peace-keeping and law enforcement responsibilities as an equal partner. At times, especially when dealing with people who need highly specialized help, it becomes your prime duty.

FORCE AND DISCRETION

The law allows you to use force in your work.[3] It does so for the reason that force is impossible to avoid in some of your jobs, such as the arrest of a resisting and angry suspect or the effort to end a barroom brawl. But the law requires that you always exert the least amount of force possible—just enough to protect yourself and successfully end the problem at hand.

If you use a greater amount of force than is warranted, you leave yourself open to charges of assaulting the person with whom you are dealing and can be taken to court for doing so. The rule concerning the least amount of force necessary does not apply to the police alone. It applies to all citizens.

You are also allowed to use discretion in your dealings with people.[4] Discretion customarily plays a part only in the settling of minor problems. It sees you put your good judgment to work rather than follow the exact letter of the law. For example, suppose you apprehend an eleven-year-old girl as she is shoplifting a bar of candy. Instead of taking

her to juvenile hall, you return her to her parents, discuss the matter with them, and impress the seriousness of her offense on the youngster; you are using your discretion. You choose these steps because you feel they will accomplish more good than would some hours or a night among other, possibly very hardened, juvenile offenders.

You can use your discretion in many other ways. For instance, instead of handing out a citation for parking in a no-parking zone, you listen to a woman driver's reasons for stopping there and then send her off with a warning not to repeat the offense.

Discretion is employed for several reasons. First, it can quickly solve a minor problem and allow you to get on with your work. Second, it avoids penalizing a minor offender with a punishment that will benefit neither the offender nor the general public. Finally, in many instances, your kindness enhances the reputation of your department and police officers everywhere. You come off as an understanding human being rather than an automaton who works coldly by the "rule book."

However, you are not allowed to give your discretion full rein. The amount permitted will be set by the operating policies of your department. For example, suppose that you come upon two twelve-year-olds smoking marijuana. One department might allow you two choices in the matter: to take them into custody or, if you think a talk with their parents will serve better, escort them home. But another department may give you just one choice: to take them into custody and place them in the care of the juvenile authorities.

Armed and helmeted California Highway Patrol officers seem to be using excessive force in arresting an unarmed demonstrator in Concord, California, in 1987.

PUBLIC CRITICISM

In all, your various responsibilities make your role in society both a complex and demanding one. It is also a role that is sharply criticized by great segments of the world public—and has been sharply criticized for centuries now. Throughout your career in uniform, you'll hear the police charged with various failures and misdeeds. Here are three of the most widely heard complaints.

1. *The police are supposed to fight crime. They are doing a poor job.* Here in the United States, critics of the police substantiate this charge by pointing to the nation's annual crime rate. It has shown a pretty steady increase over the past fifteen to twenty years. It reached its peak in 1980, lingered at about the same level in 1981, and dipped between 1982 and 1984. But it began to rise again in 1985. According to the Federal Bureau of Investigation, some 12,430,000 crimes were reported that year, an increase of 548,000 over the number in 1984.[5] In many minds, these figures leave no doubt that the police are failing as crime fighters.

2. *The police misuse their authority. They are guilty of acts of brutality against members of the public.* Here, the critics point to such cases as that of a Detroit black man. In 1978, an undercover police team stopped his car while investigating the kidnapping of women at bus stops. The man sued the police for taking him from behind the wheel and beating him so severely that he suffered permanent brain damage. In 1987, a jury decided that his story was true and awarded him more than $1 million in damages.[6]

3. *The police abuse their authority in yet another way. They themselves can be as corrupt as the worst of criminals.* Again, there are cases to substantiate this criticism. In early 1987, for example, seven officers with Florida's Miami Police Department were accused of racketeering and drug

possession. The accusation came after the seven had descended on a band of drug smugglers unloading a shipment of cocaine from a small boat. The smugglers, attempting to escape, dove over the side and drowned. The officers were charged with then keeping the cocaine and selling it for a multimillion-dollar profit.[7]

Though the most often heard, these three charges are far from being the only ones leveled against the police. There are also accusations that you and your fellow officers harass the poor and members of minority groups; that you give more service to the wealthy and the well-to-do than to the poor; and that you have made yourselves feared strangers to the public by donning military-type uniforms and riding around in cruisers rather than walking your beat and getting to know the people there.

A MIXED PICTURE

If you're a good officer, these criticisms will hurt and anger you. You'll know that you—and countless policemen and -women like you—are doing the best and most honorable job you can. But, in all honesty, you'll also know that many of your fellow officers are failing in their duties. Perhaps they are careless or lazy, perhaps they are bullies, perhaps they are prejudiced toward some of the people they are supposed to be serving, perhaps their uniform has made them officious, perhaps they are dishonest and thus vulnerable to taking graft.

As you look at your department, you'll come to understand one thing above all else. It is like any other organization. It is made up of human beings, all of whom are capable of error. Some of its personnel are efficient, dedicated to doing the best job possible, and wise in their dealings with everyone, from the most innocent citizen to the guiltiest of suspects. Others are what the police them-

29

selves describe as "bad apples," who give the rest of you and your role in society a tarnished reputation.

But there is another side to the picture. You'll learn other things as you go along. You'll find that, while many of the criticisms are justified, many are not. You'll find, for instance, that some people regard the police as natural enemies; on being legally questioned on the street or quietly arrested for an offense, they will often try to make themselves look like innocent victims by accusing you of brutality or harassment. Conversely, you'll find that many people admire the police and their ability to put up with all sorts of ugly situations day after day. And you'll find that the police have answers for many of the criticisms leveled against them.

In all, you'll find the picture of the police and the public to be a mixed and often confusing one. It is a picture that we will try to make clear in this book.

But at this point we can say only one thing for certain. The public criticism of the police dates far back into history. We turn now to that history.

2

The Police Officer
A Hated Yesteryear

Little is known about the birth of police work. Written records of the first police either were not kept or were lost through the following centuries. We do know that in most of the world's earliest cultures law enforcement lay in the hands of kings, tribal chieftains, village councils, and priests; they made the laws and set the punishments for misdeeds. We also know that law enforcement in later ancient cultures fell much to the military. Kings and nobles maintained their own armies to keep the peace at home and in conquered lands.[1]

Today in the United States, the municipal police departments (as well as the state and federal police forces) are—and have always been—civilian organizations. They have no connection with the military. (An exception is the U.S. Coast Guard, which enforces maritime law and order along the nation's coasts; it is not only a police unit with authority over civilian activities but also a military outfit.) The various branches of the armed services operate their own police forces, all of which deal only with people in

31

uniform. The same holds true in England. But, in many nations, the ancient police ties with the military remain intact.

For example, the Greek, Italian, French, and Spanish police are linked in some manner with their nations' armies. In Italy, the police choose their recruits from young men who have served in the military with honor and distinction; the Italian police become a fighting unit when war breaks out. In France, the municipal police are organized along military lines, with soldier-policemen, called *gendarmes*; they serve the country's small cities and towns and are commanded by the minister of war. Large cities are usually served by civilian departments.[2]

THE BRITISH POLICE

England was one of the first nations to separate the police from the military.[3] In the eleventh century, the government called for each shire (county) to appoint a civilian official who would administer the local law. He was given the title *reeve*, a name that was eventually transformed into a term familiar to everyone today—*sheriff*. He was empowered to enlist members of the public in tracking down known or suspected outlaws. The public was expected to assist him without complaint because the laws of the time required that a criminal be punished by the person or persons he had harmed.

The reeve was also allowed to employ men to tend his horses. These men were known as *keepers of the stables*. Their title was soon shortened to one that applied to practically all police officers in the English-speaking world for centuries—*constable*. The term is still used in Great Britain and in many small American communities.

The next step in England's development of a civilian police force came in 1285 when the nation established a law requiring every city and town to have two constables for every one hundred citizens. In addition, the law required the cities and towns to be patrolled at night and thus be protected around the clock.

This around-the-clock system was known as the "watch and ward." Men on the watch worked at night, and the ward men during the day. Most of the watch-and-warders served without pay. Some volunteered for the work. Some were required to take turns at the job by their community leaders.

Public Complaints

Still another major development in the British police system began to take shape in the late 1700s. Out of it came some of the earliest public complaints that we have on record of the municipal police. Here is what happened.

At the time, England was witnessing the birth of the Industrial Revolution and was changing from an agricultural to a manufacturing nation. Thousands of people were leaving the hardships of poor-paying farm life and rushing to the cities in the hope of finding jobs in the factories springing up there. But, because the factories paid scant wages and because so many of the newcomers could find no work, the cities were soon infested with poverty-stricken areas—slum neighborhoods. The worst and largest of these blighted districts were to be found sprawling out for miles around the center of London.

As has always held true where living conditions are overly crowded and sordid, crimes of all sorts flourished in the London slums—everything from petty thefts to murders. The police and the courts attempted to stem the tide. The former tried to do the job with clubs and arrests, while the latter handed out a string of cruel punishments. One of the most outrageous punishments made the theft of a loaf of bread a hanging offense. In a single month near the end of the century, more than forty people were executed daily for such petty thefts.

The police and court actions did no good. The police were ineffective for two reasons. First, London was using the watch and ward system, with each neighborhood having its own unit. Each unit operated on its own and neither worked with nor cooperated with the others. The result: a highly inefficient police service.

Second, the watch-and-warders were anything but a carefully chosen lot. As usual, most worked without pay; many served unwillingly because they were forced to the task by the neighborhood leaders. The few who were paid received a meager wage and served because they were unfit for or unable to find better employment. Consequently, the men were not selected for their abilities. They were taken simply because they were sorely needed. Then they were given no training and so had no idea of how to go about the all-important job of preventing and controlling crime. They ended up being despised by the people and scorned by the criminal.

As for the courts, their harsh punishments did nothing to deter starving people from stealing food. Nor did they stop hardened criminals from thinking they could outwit the inept watch-and-warders.

And so the crime wave continued. London's jails and prisons—as was true in other cities—became so jammed with the prisoners that the courts began to deport many inmates, sending them to such distant British holdings as Australia, New Zealand, and—prior to the Revolutionary War—the American colonies. By the early 1800s, the situation in London had grown so intolerable that the public was outraged and many of the country's leaders were demanding an immediate solution.

Sir Robert Peel

One of those leaders was a high-ranking government official, Sir Robert Peel.[4] Peel attacked the London problem by first studying the police forces in other cities. They were mainly watch and ward units, and he immediately found most to be as inefficiently run and scorned as their London counterparts. Then he noted something else: he detected a connection between an area's crime rate and the quality of the local police work. The crime rate loomed highest in those areas where police efficiency and public respect were at their worst. In those few places blessed with better efficiency and greater respect, the crime rate was lower.

On the basis of his study, Peel urged a number of reforms for the London police. He called for the watch and ward units to be replaced by a single city-wide force so that all the lack of cooperation would disappear. He also wanted the new force, though a civilian agency, to be set up along military lines. This would give it a definite chain of command from top to bottom and would guarantee that everyone worked according to the same rules and orders.

As for the constables themselves, Peel saw them as the very backbone of the force as they patrolled and guarded the streets. He urged that the best men be found and trained. To get fine men, the department was to pay them a decent wage. When first recruited, they would be made to serve a probationary period and not win a permanent position until they proved themselves suitable for the work.

Peel wrote these and other ideas into a legislative bill—known as the Metropolitan Police Act—that was enacted into law by Parliament in 1828. Immediately, he was assigned the task of forming a new police department for London. He set up headquarters at Scotland Yard and began recruiting and training his officers. Prior to this time, most watch-and-warders wore their regular clothing while on duty. In keeping with one of his ideas, Peel dressed his constables in uniforms, saying that they would be more easily identifiable and would better impress the people if dressed alike. The uniform he selected consisted of a top hat and tail coat. The officers soon became known—and are still known today—as *bobbies*. The nickname was derived from Peel's first name, Robert.

Right from its start, Peel's force proved successful. The crime rate dipped in London. Public respect for the police went up. Soon, other British cities adopted Peel's ideas and began to form departments modeled on the London force. Then his ideas spread to other nations, the United States among them. With Robert Peel, the modern municipal police department was born.

THE AMERICAN POLICE

The towns of colonial America protected their streets with the old watch and ward system.[5] It won as much public scorn here as in England—and for the same reasons. It was famous for its inefficiency. All of its personnel were untrained. Most were unpaid. Many served unwillingly because they were made to do so by the town fathers. Since there was always the need for men, many towns assigned convicted criminals to watch and ward duty as a part of their punishment. The system finally went out of style in the early 1800s.

It was then that the growth of the nation's cities brought about the need for better police service—a paid service. In 1833, Philadelphia hired its first salaried daytime constables (a watch, principally volunteer, worked at night). At the start, the department was headed by a captain, who was appointed by the mayor. Some years later, it was placed under a chief of police. He, too, was appointed by the mayor.

Other cities soon followed in Philadelphia's footsteps. Boston, while continuing to use a volunteer watch shift, established a paid day force of six men in 1838. Six years later, New York City, after studying Peel's London department, abolished the various independent watch and ward groups that had long guarded its many neighborhoods. They were replaced by a single department that served the entire city day and night. New York became the first U.S.

36

city with a single around-the-clock police department based on Peel's ideas.

Similar departments quickly took shape—in Chicago (1851), New Orleans and Cincinnati (1852), and Baltimore (1857). By the end of the Civil War, the municipal police force had been born in most of the nation's major cities and was struggling to grow into the organized department that it is today.

Problem Years

Struggling is the right word to describe that growth. While the new departments were an improvement over the old watch and ward system, they were for years in the 1800s burdened with two problems that earned them widespread contempt.

First, the departments were held in low regard because the public had not yet forgotten its dislike of the watch-and-warders. This made it difficult for them to recruit capable officers. The result: too often, men able to find jobs elsewhere turned up their noses at police work, and the departments were left to hire the poorest and most scorned of the immigrants pouring into the country at the time— all of which did nothing but add to the lack of public respect. Second, for much of the century, the police, especially those in the nation's largest cities, were the victims of corrupt political interference.[6] In many instances, they were willing victims.

At the time, almost every department was contolled by the politicians who held power in its city. The politicians unfailingly used the department to their advantage. They hired the officers and chief, choosing relatives and cronies for the posts. They made sure that they and their friends were immune from arrest for any misdeed. They demanded that the department always "look the other way" when they dealt in graft and other shady operations. Honest officers who dared complain about what they saw could count on being discharged. To hold on to their jobs and save their families from starving, most good officers simply kept their mouths shut.

In fairness, it must be said that not every city politician of the day was dishonest. But far too many were. And, whether honest or corrupt, practically all of them practiced the age-old military motto of "To the victor go the spoils of war," with one of their chief spoils (rewards) being the control of the city's law enforcement unit. It was a widespread custom of the times that still plagues some cities today. Consequently, the department suffered a lack of competent and well-trained men.

Many, on being hired, were thrust onto the streets or dropped behind desks without any preparation or any real understanding of their jobs. Many were lazy and not interested in police work but only in the salary that their politically won posts gave them. Ill-chosen and untrained, some were brutes who took pleasure in mistreating suspects and prisoners. Some were as dishonest as the politicians who hired them. They engaged in graft—went "on the take"—pocketing money for ignoring the criminal enterprises around them and for providing an extra bit of protection for the businesses on their beat.

On top of all else, most city forces, because of the political control and because they were still so young, had not yet developed firm standards of officer performance and conduct. Even the best chiefs had no workable system for controlling or disciplining the "bad apples" under them. Consequently, officer drunkenness was widespread. Attacks on superior officers were common. The cruel treatment of suspects and prisoners was an everyday fact of life. Nationwide, the police were regarded as brutish political hirelings who knew nothing about their jobs.

A New Development

All this corruption did not trouble only the cities. It also plagued the state and federal governments. By late in the century, it had infuriated Americans everywhere, among them scores of fair-minded civic, state, and national leaders. The anger eventually led to a major development in 1883—the passage of the Pendleton Act by Congress. Authored by Senator George Hunt Pendleton of Ohio, the Act was intended to take all levels of public employment— police work among them—out from under the thumbs of politicians.

It did so by establishing for federal workers what is known as the Civil Service Commission. The Commission was empowered to recruit thousands of federal workers through open, competitive examinations. In a single stroke, the Act and its Commission ended the hiring and firing of employees on the basis of their political connections. Ability and merit became the criteria for getting and holding a job.

Because it was a federal measure, the Act applied only to federal employees. But within months of its passage, as Pendleton had hoped, the states began to follow with civil service programs of their own. New York was the first state to take action. The New York City Police Department became the first municipal force to operate under the civil service system.

Today, some 95 percent of all federal, state, county, and city employees work within the system, with their applications for jobs and the jobs themselves protected from political interference and dependent on performance only. Cities and counties that do not operate under the system usually have what are called *merit ordinances*. These ordinances are laws that accomplish the same ends as the system itself by requiring that employment be always based on ability.

Political–Police Corruption:
A Slow Death

With the arrival of the civil service system, the municipal forces were freed from political control in their hiring practices. But this does not mean that all political control came to an abrupt end. The politicians in power continued to exercise much influence, especially among the chiefs and high-ranking officers. For years to come, such major cities as Chicago, New York, Detroit, and Los Angeles were to be rocked by reports of political–police corruption.

For example, on an Election Day in Chicago during the late 1920s, officers were forced to hand out circulars in favor of the candidates supported by the political party in power.[7] In the 1930s, police and politicians in San Francisco and Detroit were accused of belonging to gambling and prostitution rings.[8] In the 1960s, Chicago learned that a high-ranking police official allowed a gambling ring to operate in his district on orders from a local political leader; the officer received a share of the ring's profits for his co-operation.[9] At the same time, the city heard that one of its most prominent politicians had made a trip to Arizona to obtain a large sum of money put up by a crime syndicate to insure that a certain police lieutenant would be promoted to the rank of captain.[10]

Early on, scandals such as these led angry citizens to call for police reform in their cities. As well as witnessing the birth of the civil service system, the late 1800s saw a growing number of cities elect political candidates who were dedicated to cleaning up their police forces. Joined by honest police officials, these reformers did much to break up the long-standing political–police corruption. They also brought about better methods of policing and department organization.

As a result of this reform work and the civil service system, the municipal department was improved and its officers began to win an increasing degree of public respect. Many city police forces were slowly transformed into the well-organized and respected units that they are today. But political–police corruption was to die a slow death and, to this day, remains alive in a number of major cities. It has, however, virtually disappeared in other cities, one of them said to be the once scandal-ridden Los Angeles.

TOWARD TODAY

The remaining history that brings us to the modern police department was made up not only of the reform work and the civil service system. There were other equally important developments. Some came in the late nineteenth century and some in the twentieth. Among the most significant were the following:

As the cities grew over the years and encountered the increasing criminal and peace-keeping problems that growth invariably brings, the departments added to their personnel. Increasingly sought was the number of officers needed to provide adequate protection at a tax cost acceptable to the public. Overall, in today's cities and towns, that number—known as the police-citizen ratio—averages 2.6 police employees (officers and other workers) per 1,000 citizens.[11]

One of the most significant developments came in the late nineteenth century. It was then that the New York City department realized there were police jobs that women wanted to do and felt entitled to do. They were jobs that would free male officers for street duty and jobs that were better suited for a woman than a man. In 1884, the department hired the nation's first policewomen, assigning them to clerical work and to cases involving women, young girls, and children.[12] As we all know, women today are no longer limited to such duties. They are doing the same jobs that men have long handled.

The passing years also witnessed a parade of scientific and mechanical developments that proved to be of value to the departments. Fingerprinting, though known in China and elsewhere centuries ago, came into widespread use as an investigative and records-keeping tool in the early 1900s. It was followed by such other major aids as the polygraph (lie detector); the camera and roll film; the automobile; aircraft; radio and television; and, most recently, the computer. All these developments challenged the police to work successfully with them and necessitated the

Police work now utilizes sophisticated technology.

hiring of certain personnel that no one in an earlier age had dreamed of—among them, laboratory technicians, radio dispatchers, auto mechanics, and helicopter pilots.

Likewise, the problems endured by twentieth-century cities brought the need for still other new personnel. For example, the widespread public use of the automobile led the departments to develop units solely for traffic control. The mounting drug abuse late in the century saw some officers assigned exclusively to drug investigations.

The beginning employment of women officers in the late nineteenth century had marked a great development in police work. Another major development came in the twentieth century and was ushered in by the civil rights movement of the 1950s. Ever since, there has been a campaign to employ greater numbers of minority officers. It is a campaign that has been urged along by leaders in the nation's growing minority populations; they want their people to share in a work that had previously been limited to whites.

It is also a campaign that has been met with mixed reactions by the police. Some departments have willingly taken part in it because they realize that minority members can make good officers and because they understand that a minority officer can often do a better job than a white when dealing with the people in a minority neighborhood. Some departments have balked at the campaign—often out of a long-standing sense of prejudice—and have been forced to participate by the nation's fair-employment laws.

As a result of these developments—and many others— we today have come closer than ever before to what can be called the ideal municipal department—the department that, no matter whether it be in a big city or small town, is well organized and equipped, that meets its myriad responsibilities with fairness and calm efficiency, and that adheres to Robert Peel's belief that all its officers must be carefully selected and well trained if they are to serve the public as effectively and professionally as possible.

Let's look now at how your department is actually organized to meet its responsibilities and how you are selected and trained to take your place in it. As careful and as thorough as that selection and training attempts to be, you'll find that it has earned a goodly share of public criticism.

Officer and Department Organization and Training

At the time this book is being written, approximately 620,000 men and women work in law enforcement at the municipal, county, and state levels. Of that total, the greatest number serve with municipal departments—more than 392,000. They work in departments of varying size. Their departments range in manpower from one or two officers in small towns to the legions found in the nation's largest cities—25,000, for example, in New York City. (The New York figure refers only to actual officers and does not include such civilian employees as mechanics and many office workers.)[1]

Regardless of size, their departments are alike in several ways. They are all agencies that are answerable only to the local government and public for their actions and aims. While they must obey the U.S. Constitution and their state constitutions, they are in no way governed by the federal and state authorities. This independence from higher levels of government makes them quite different from many municipal departments elsewhere. Often the departments in other countries are branches of the national government or are connected with it in some way. You'll recall that the police in some nations are linked with the military.

Further, after years of experience, the departments, from the smallest to the largest, are all organized to one degree or another; each is headed by one officer—a chief of police or someone of an equivalent position—who is responsible for all aspects of the department's activities. The exact manner of organization depends on a department's size. It is at its simplest in those small towns that need but a handful of officers. It grows steadily more complex as departments increase in size.

But, no matter a department's size, it is organized around six basic areas of police work: street patrol; criminal investigation; inspection of local buildings for such problems as safety code violations; services to and the training of personnel; maintenance of facilities and equipment; and department planning and development. Also placed within the organizational setup are such specialized services as those supplied by bomb squads, hostage negotiators, and Special Weapons and Tactics (SWAT) teams.

In small departments, these various work areas are usually shared by all the officers, with an individual officer perhaps taking on two or three of them. For instance, an officer may be assigned to daily patrol duty and also to department planning and criminal investigations. Larger departments, however, split themselves into units, with each unit being responsible for one particular area. The units are called divisions. Each division breaks the areas of work within it into what are called sections. In still larger departments, some of the divisions are placed together in what are known as bureaus.

All municipal forces maintain a central headquarters. A large city department, because it embraces a broad geographical area, usually divides its territory into smaller areas, called precincts or districts. Each precinct or district has a headquarters of its own and is headed by a ranking officer. All precincts work under the direction of the central headquarters. In some cities, each precinct provides complete police service—from street patrols to criminal investigations. In others, the precincts provide just one or two services. They perhaps handle street patrols and traffic control, while criminal investigations are conducted by detectives from central headquarters.

Now let's say that you want to be a municipal police officer. You'll go through a number of steps to be selected and then trained for a job in uniform. As you do so, you'll run into the first of the public criticisms that you'll encounter throughout your career. Some of the selection and training procedures have come under fire from many people.

JOINING THE DEPARTMENT

Whether male or female, you must show yourself to be physically, mentally, emotionally, and morally fit before being hired.[2] Ordinarily, you must be at least twenty-one years of age and usually no older than thirty-one to thirty-five. A few departments accept candidates as young as eighteen or nineteen. And a few have no top age limit.

Physically, you must have near-perfect eyesight without corrective lenses. Your height and weight must be in proper proportion. This proportion is required because studies have shown that overweight officers run such health risks as high blood pressure and heart attack when up against the rigors of directing traffic for hours at a time or pursuing a suspect on foot.

There was a time when most departments set a minimum weight and height for male officers, with the minimum weight running at about 145 pounds. The minimum height was usually 5 feet 7 inches. At the opposite end of the spectrum, you could ordinarily be no taller than 6 feet 5 inches to 6 feet 7 inches. The minimum weight-height

47

was established on the basis that smallish men would have difficulty when dealing with suspects who overshadowed and outweighed them.

These physical minimums bring us to the first of the public criticisms you'll encounter. In recent years, the minimums have been challenged by applicants and segments of the public on the grounds that they excluded too many good people from entering police work. By itself, the minimum height of 5 feet 7 inches kept more than 97 percent of all American women and 45 percent of all U.S. males from joining the departments. The challenge has borne fruit. Because of it, the minimums are now rarely ever applied to women and are used only here and there for men. Replacing them is the demand for a proper proportion between weight and height.

Various measurements are used to determine the acceptable proportion—for example, comparisons of your weight with the size of your bones or frame. Widely employed are medical charts that call for a certain weight range at a given height. To see how such a chart works, suppose that you're a woman applicant who stands 5 feet tall. Depending on such factors as bone structure, you'll need to weigh between 102 and 122 pounds. If, on the other hand, you're an inch over 6 feet tall, your weight will have to run between 149 and 173 pounds.

In addition to meeting the physical standards, you must have a background clean of felony convictions. You must be able to read and write efficiently. Graduation from high school is demanded by most police agencies. Many departments require two to four years of college education; some departments prefer that your college education include courses in police science and criminology; a few require such courses. If you've served in the military, an honorable discharge is essential. You must be a citizen of the United States.

To determine your overall fitness for police work, the department will examine you closely. You'll be given phys-

*Police officers today come in
different shapes and sizes.*

ical and psychiatric examinations. You'll be checked for physical agility. You'll be interviewed by superior officers, individually and then in a group known as an *orals board*. Your past life will be investigated, and you'll sit for a polygraph (lie detector) test concerning your background. You'll also sit for a civil service or similar test. Then, on meeting the various standards and being accepted by the department, you'll be hired as a probationary officer and begin your training.

TRAINING

If you're joining a big-city force, it will likely have its own training school—the police academy. Small departments usually do not maintain academies. Rather, they send their recruits to a nearby city academy or to a training center that serves the departments within a given region.

On arriving at the academy or center, you'll be given a training uniform. You'll also be issued your badge—your *shield*—with your identification number on it.

The police uniform has an interesting history. Most of the first paid officers did not wear uniforms. This was because they were ashamed of their profession and did not want to be recognized as officers unless they had to identify themselves in the line of duty. Their embarrassment stemmed from the fact that, as you'll recall, the public did not look on police work as a respectable occupation because of the poor reputation earned by the early watch-and-warders.

By the 1850s, however, the city departments were realizing that a uniform of some sort was needed and had begun to have their men at least wear identical hats or helmets. At mid-decade, New York City adopted the use of a full uniform. The same uniform, however, was not worn throughout the city; each precinct selected its own style. The next years saw other departments opt in favor of a uniform. By the 1860s, most departments were calling for their officers to wear an outfit consisting of dark trousers and coat, badge, and helmet. The helmet, similar to the high-domed headgear still employed in Great Britain, was widely worn until 1901, when it was replaced by the first of today's regulation caps.

The shield also has an interesting history. The United States is one of a very few nations in which it is worn. It came into use in the late 1800s when the city departments were under the thumb of corrupt politicians. Along with the poor reputation left over from the watch and ward days, the situation so shamed many good officers that they did not want to be known as policemen. They refused to wear their uniforms. Instead, they began to carry a badge beneath their civilian clothing, suspending it from their necks by means of a cord or ribbon. Then, when needing to identify themselves, they would produce the badge. When the establishment of the civil service system at last made police work respectable, the uniform returned to fashion and the badge became a part of it.[3]

Many historians believe that today's widely used nickname for officers—cop—can be traced back to the New York City policemen of the 1800s. They carried a copper badge and were soon familiarly known as coppers, with that nickname eventually being abbreviated to cop. There is also the belief that cop may have come from the manner in which officers of the late 1800s and early 1900s signed the department log book when reporting for work. On signing, each officer would follow his name with the words "Constable on Patrol."

Today, the municipal uniform varies from state to state in style and color. Regardless of the variations, you'll carry the same equipment as a fellow officer elsewhere. You'll wear your shield and carry one or two whistles; if two are required, one will be used for controlling traffic, and the other for summoning fellow officers. You'll also carry a notebook, pen, pencil, handcuffs, and a baton (nightstick). Around your waist you'll wear a gunbelt and a holster for

New York City transit
police officer with
gun, nightstick, and
walkie-talkie

your sidearm. Your sidearm will be a revolver or a semi-automatic pistol of a caliber determined by the department.

The uniform brings us to another criticism. Many people feel that some police garb—black leather jackets, boots, and helmets—gives officers a hard look that angers and frightens rather than creates a public liking and trust. A number of departments have heeded this criticism and have altered their uniforms accordingly.

Weapons Training

Early in your training, you'll be instructed in the use of your sidearm (and other weapons). You'll be taught how to handle it carefully and skillfully and fire it with accuracy. As to when you should pull the gun, you'll be told to employ it always with discretion and to draw it only in circumstances when you think its use is absolutely necessary.

Target practice

But just what are those circumstances? The gun policy of the New York City Police provides a good example of what you will be told. As an NYPD officer, you may not fire a gun to stop a suspect or prevent a crime unless you are faced with either of two circumstances: (1) you have good reason to think that you yourself, a fellow officer, or an innocent citizen may be killed by the suspect if you fail to act, or (2) you have a good reason to think that you have no other "reasonable means" for making the arrest or stopping the crime. You are even prohibited from cocking your gun until the last possible moment.[4]

You'll also be instructed that the weapon is to be carried at all times, even when you are off-duty. This is because you will be required to take action whenever you come across a crime or a criminal. (Depending on your department's policies, you may not be required to carry the weapon while away on vacation.) In all the years to come, you will perhaps never have to fire a shot, but throughout your career—no matter how high you rise in the department—you will be made to repeat your weapons training to see that your care and skill remain intact.

And now we come to yet another public criticism: despite the training given officers, many Americans have long feared the misuse of the gun by their police. They have had good reason for their fears. Over the years, the press has reported numerous police shootings for reasons ranging from the officer's acting too quickly to outright viciousness. In California during the 1960s, for instance, an officer on night patrol came across a burglar fleeing a store. When the suspect failed to stop on being commanded to do so, the officer drew his gun and fired a warning shot. The officer later said that the shot was aimed above the suspect's head. But the bullet struck the suspect in the back and killed him. The burglar turned out to be an unarmed twelve-year-old who had stolen a few dollars' worth of food. The shooting was judged to have been unnecessary.[5]

A shock wave went through San Antonio, Texas, in

54

1986 when a city patrolman was said to be implicated in a string of "vigilante-type" killings of suspected or known criminals. The matter came to light when a local newspaper reported that a young man had been murdered by four shots fired from an alley 75 feet away as he was burglarizing a truck. The paper hinted that the killer was a police officer. The San Antonio department launched an investigation of the suspected patrolman but had to put it aside for lack of evidence. Then the suspect was shot and killed by a fellow patrolman. The fellow officer claimed that he had acted in self-defense after his friend had pulled a gun and had threatened to kill him because he "knew too much." Since then, the dead officer has again been under investigation. He is suspected of having participated in at least six vigilante-type murders.[6]

Incidents such as these, while shocking the entire nation, have especially alarmed many of the people who want to see the use of guns, particularly handguns, banned in the United States.[7] They would like the ban extended not only to the general public but to the police as well. Their arguments are many. For one, they contend that the police gun is a threat to the public safety when it is drawn by an angry officer or an officer filled with fear by an ugly arrest situation. For another, there is the belief that the police gun invites a violent reaction on the parts of suspects and criminals when faced with it. The critics of the police gun say that U.S. would be wise to imitate such countries as Great Britain, where the police, except in special circumstances, are forbidden to carry firearms and have long worked successfully without them.

While agreeing that the gun is dangerous, the police—and much of the public—disagree with these arguments. They argue that many, if not most, criminals are known to carry guns (or other weapons) to protect themselves from their rivals and the police and to intimidate their victims. So far as intimidation is concerned, armed robbers are prime cases in point. They use the gun to frighten a victim

55

into doing what they want, and doing it quickly. The police contend that it would be unfair and suicidal to send unarmed officers up against such offenders.

They also feel it is unfair to expect their officers to go unarmed because the officers in another nation do so. It is true, they agree, that the long-standing British police tradition of not carrying weapons has helped to create a similar tradition among the nation's criminals. Knowing that they are not up against an armed foe—and knowing that heavy penalties are exacted for armed crimes—they have tended not to arm themselves. But the tradition here in the United States is vastly different. From the days of our earliest settlers, the gun has always been widely owned. As a result, though our penalties for armed offenses can be heavy, American criminals long ago grew accustomed to carrying weapons. The time may come when this American tradition is changed and the criminal no longer feels it wise or "macho" to use a gun. But the police believe that time will be long in coming, if indeed it ever arrives. In the meantime, they argue that it is, again, suicidal to ask their officers to disarm themselves.

In defending their use of the gun, the police claim that it is presently being employed with greater care than in the past. They substantiate this claim by pointing to statistics dating back to the early 1970s. The figures show that, in 1971 alone, 350 people were killed by officers in fifty of the nation's largest cities; the annual number of killings was down to 172 in the mid-1980s. In New York City, 314 were killed between 1970 and 1974; 173 died at police hands between 1980 and 1984. In the first five years of the 1970s, fatal police shootings were responsible for 4 percent of all New York City homicides; during the first five years of the 1980s, such shootings accounted for 2 percent of the city's homicides.[8]

Though any death by gunfire is to be deplored, the police say bluntly that killing often cannot be avoided in arrests involving violence or violent resistance. They are pleased with the shrinking death rate and credit several factors for the decline. Among them are improved training methods; increased officer caution due to the growing number of lawsuits being brought against the police by wounded parties or the families of those killed; department investigations of all intentional and unintentional gun firings; and punishments for all unwarranted and accidental firings. Accidental gun discharges often bring reprimands and the requirement that extra weapons training be taken. Unwarranted firings can result in dismissal from the force or suspensions without pay for a number of days or weeks.

Department Policies

At the outset of your training, you'll be given your department's manual of policies governing officer performance and behavior. Adherence to these policies is necessary on two counts—to do your job as the department knows it must be done and to avoid departmental charges of misconduct and the possibility of dismissal from the force.

The manual will touch many areas of your personal as well as your professional life. It will prohibit you, for example, from associating with racketeers, gamblers, and known criminals except in the line of duty. You'll never be allowed to take an alcoholic drink while on duty; nor, when off-duty, will you be permitted to drink to the point where you are unfit for a quick return to work. You'll also be required to have department approval before accepting a reward. The same goes for any gift or award connected in any way with your job performance.

Physical and Paramedical Training

So that you'll be prepared to meet any crisis, some of your schooling will be given to physical and paramedical training. The former will include lessons in the martial arts, with the emphasis on defensive rather than attack techniques. As an officer, remember, you'll be required by law never to bully a suspect or use undue force when making an arrest; as we'll see later, it is a requirement that many people accuse the police of too-often ignoring. You'll also learn the proper way to drive a car, vault a fence, rush up a fire escape, climb bridges and their cables, and rescue a drowning person. Your paramedical training will see you coached in the rudiments of first-aid care for the sick and injured.

THE OATH OF OFFICE

On successfully completing your training, you will take the oath of office. You'll swear or affirm always to follow certain precepts throughout your career. These precepts are usually contained in a simple and brief statement. Though the oaths differ in some detail from city to city, they are generally similar to the example below:

> I, _____ , do solemnly swear that I will support the Constitution of the United States, and the Constitution of (name of state), and that I will faithfully discharge the duties of a police officer for the city of _____ , according to the best of my ability. So help me God.[9]

In addition to their oath of office, many officers live by what is called the Law Enforcement Code of Ethics. In some cities, the Code of Ethics has replaced the oath or has been incorporated into it. The Code was developed in 1955 by two organizations dedicated to improving law enforcement work—the California Peace Officers Association and the Peace Officers Research Association. It has since been adopted by many law enforcement agencies across the country. It reads:

AS A LAW ENFORCEMENT OFFICER, my fundamental duty is to mankind; to safeguard lives and property; to protect the innocent against deception, the weak against oppression and intimidation, and the peaceful against violence and disorder; to respect the Constitutional rights of all men to liberty, equality, and justice.

I WILL keep my private life unsullied as an example to all; maintain courageous calm in the face of danger, scorn, or ridicule; develop self-restraint; and be consistently mindful of the welfare of others. I will be exemplary in obeying the laws of the land and the regulations of my department. Whatever I see or hear of a confidential nature, or that is confided to me in my official capacity, will be kept secret unless revelation is necessary in the performance of my duty.

I WILL never act officiously or permit personal feelings, prejudices, animosities, or friendships to influence my decisions. With no compromise for crime and with relentless prosecution of criminals, I will enforce the law courteously and appropriately without fear or favor, malice, or ill-will, never employing unnecessary force or violence and never accepting gratuities.

I RECOGNIZE the badge of my office as a symbol of public faith, and I accept it as a public trust to be held so long as I am true to the ethics of police service. I will constantly strive to achieve these objectives and ideals, dedicating myself before God to my chosen profession—law enforcement.[10]

FUTURE TRAINING

Your training does not end with your academy graduation. It will continue throughout your career. You'll participate in in-service programs; taught by superior officers or members of the department's training unit, they will cover matters ranging from new police techniques to changes in the law. And you'll find *roll-call training* to be widely used. It usually consists of ten-minute instructional periods that are held between the time that officers arrive for work and depart for the field.

On graduation from the academy, you'll be given the rank of patrolman. You may wish to remain in this rank, which constitutes the backbone of any department, for your entire career. Or you may wish to go on to higher ranks, doing so by taking advanced training and passing examinations. Or you may want to move into—or be assigned to—a particular work area. Perhaps you'll specialize in criminal investigation or drug enforcement, or perhaps become a member of a bomb squad or SWAT team. In all instances, you will require special training.

*   *   *

And so your initial training is at an end. You've taken your oath of office and are ready for work. In the next chapters, we'll talk about that work and the problems and public criticisms that have long surrounded it. We'll begin with the demands that will be made on you by the laws and legal precepts contained in the basic documents under which we all live—the Constitution of the United States and the Bill of Rights.

Officer and Department
Basic Laws, Public Complaints

Everyone in the United States lives under local, state, and federal laws. Of these laws, the most fundamental and over-riding are to be found in the nation's Constitution and Bill of Rights. Both set forth the legal principles under which the country operates. All state constitutions must be in keeping with them. All laws enacted at any level of government must not violate their principles. Because they embody the supreme law of the land and will be with you daily in your work as a police officer, the Constitution and the Bill of Rights are to be the subjects of this chapter.

THE U.S. CONSTITUTION
AND THE BILL OF RIGHTS

The U.S. Constitution does not provide for the establishment of local law enforcement agencies such as the municipal police.[1] Rather, it entrusts to the states, counties, cities, and towns the task of passing laws for the police protection of their people. To the government in Washington falls the job of creating police agencies needed at the federal level. Local police agencies, though empowered to maintain the public order and enforce the law, may not violate the precepts of the Constitution when doing so.

While not itself providing for specific local police forces, the Constitution does contain several provisions that relate to local law enforcement. For instance, there is Section 9 of Article 1. In part, the Section pertains to what is called a *writ of habeas corpus* and says that a citizen's privilege to this writ may not be suspended. *Habeas corpus* means "produce the body." The writ is a legal order that brings accused persons into open court to hear the charges against them and to set a date for a trial. The constitutional demand for the use of the writ prevents law enforcement agencies from holding anyone in custody indefinitely without the benefit of a courtroom appearance.

The Bill of Rights, which was adopted in 1791, contains the ten original amendments to the Constitution. Other amendments to the Constitution have been made since the Bill's passage, and the total now stands at twenty-six. For the most part, the amendments refer to the inalienable rights enjoyed by the American people. The Fourth Amendment, for instance, safeguards us against unlawful searches and seizures (arrests). The Fifth Amendment protects us from being forced to make incriminating statements against ourselves.

Because it deals with our personal rights, the Bill plays a more direct part in a police officer's life than does the Constitution as a whole. It serves as a major guideline for police procedure and conduct when maintaining the public order and enforcing the law. As an officer, you'll deal with several of its amendments throughout your career. Let's now look at three of its most important provisions and at the public criticism that is heard when the police actually violate—or are suspected of violating—them.

The First Amendment

The First Amendment concerns our basic freedoms, among them the freedom of speech and assembly. Everyone—from

62

members of religious groups and political parties to street-corner orators—has the right to speak out and assemble a crowd. People may assemble for the purposes of a peaceful strike, parade, or meeting so long as they avoid certain actions and intentions. They may not, for instance, trespass on private property or damage personal property. Nor may they gather with the idea of committing a crime. And remember that word *peaceful*. No one may speak to a crowd with the aim of inciting a riot, committing a treasonable act against the government, or overthrowing the government itself. All are deemed to be acts of unlawful assembly.

The police walk a tightrope in honoring the amendment's provision for the freedom of assembly. This is because a very thin line often separates speech that is spirited and heated from speech that is intended to incite an audience to riot. To help cut down on possible problems, many cities have a regulation requiring a license to speak before a crowd. The licensing of a speaker is, for the most part, automatic, but it does provide a way to screen potential troublemakers and thus be ready for whatever difficulties they threaten.

There are no definitive constitutional rules on which to judge whether a speech is an expression of freedom or a vehicle for causing trouble. And so, when granting or rejecting a license to speak, the police are guided by their city's law enforcement policies and the decisions of the U.S. Supreme Court in cases involving the freedoms of speech and assembly. Then, when on duty at a public gathering, officers are required to honor the Constitution by basing their control of the crowd on its actual behavior and that of the speaker and not on their own personal feelings. For example, suppose you find yourself on duty at a gathering sponsored by a religious or political group that you like or support. You may not allow the speakers to incite a riot just because you agree with what they are saying. Nor may you do nothing or barely nothing to restore order when a crowd riots against a speaker you dislike.

Over the years, many people have accused the police of First Amendment violations. One often heard complaint centers on the issuance of licenses for public assemblies. It holds that cities and the police often refuse a license to a group simply because of a dislike for members of the group or for what it represents. Many such complaints have come from minority, homosexual, and neo-Nazi organizations. (Neo-Nazis are dedicated to the racist and anti-Semitic ideas of Adolf Hitler.)

It is difficult to say when cities and their police have acted with or without good reason in refusing licenses in these cases. The applicants and the officials are always able to offer what seem to be reasonable arguments on behalf of their respective positions. On one side of the fence, the police often hold that an obvious public hostility toward a group—and not their own personal dislike—is mainly responsible for rejecting a license application. They contend that the group will attract crowds of angry citizens and make the outbreak of violence more than a possibility.

On the other side of the fence, the groups argue that a license refusal violates their right to assemble and speak freely. They say that the police are not fortune-tellers and have no way of really knowing whether one public assembly, any more than another, runs a particular risk of violence.

An incident that earned headlines across the country and made Americans everywhere aware of the arguments on both sides of the fence occurred in Illinois some years ago.[2] It took shape when the American Nazi Party (the National Socialist Party of America) sent a letter to several Chicago suburban areas, among them the Skokie and Marquette Park districts. The Party wanted to demonstrate in favor of white supremacy on April 20, 1978—the eighty-ninth anniversary of Adolf Hitler's birth—and requested a license to hold a rally. Most of the recipients ignored the letter. But Skokie officials, mindful of the rights granted by the First Amendment, informed the Party that it could hold it's rally—but only if it posted a bond in the amount of

64

$350,000 to pay for any damages that might result. Skokie was the home of many Jewish people who had suffered in Hitler's concentration camps before and during World War II. The town officials knew there would be a local outcry against the Nazis that could well erupt into violence, and so, while not refusing their permission outright, they hoped the Party would be unable to pay the bond and would seek a license elsewhere.

The Party, however, took Skokie to court and sued on the grounds that the Nazis' right to free speech was being violated. Also sued was Marquette Park, which had likewise ordered a bond. The court decided in the Party's favor in both cases and said that the demand for the bonds must be dropped. The two districts issued licenses for the rallies. In the end, the Party decided not to meet in Skokie and assembled in Marquette instead.

The rally lasted for less than an hour and was attended by twenty-five Party members. They were surrounded by a crowd of about 2,000 people. It was made up of both Nazi supporters and opponents, plus several hundred plainclothes police officers. The officers broke up a number of fistfights and arrested seventy-two people, mostly on charges of disorderly conduct.

Let's turn now from the matter of licenses to another major complaint. There has been much criticism over the years of how the police have dispersed assemblies that have been deemed unlawful for one reason or another—perhaps because they were not licensed, perhaps because they endangered private property. In the 1930s, military units and club-wielding police were used to oust workers who had taken over factories during labor strikes. The 1960s saw the police repeatedly accused of brutality when they broke up anti–Vietnam War demonstrations.

The sharpest criticism of police behavior during the Vietnam era was heard at the 1968 Democratic Convention in Chicago.[3] While the delegates in the convention hall were naming their presidential and vice-presidential candidates (Vice-President Hubert H. Humphrey and Maine

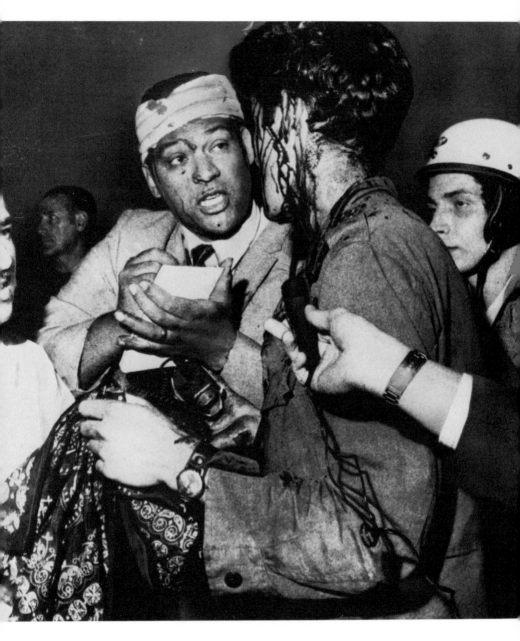

Newsman bloodied by police at the 1968
Democratic National Convention, held in Chicago

senator Edmund Muskie respectively), more than 5,000 people milled about outside. The crowd was made up of bystanders, news reporters, and anti-Vietnam protestors who supported the peace candidacy of Minnesota senator Eugene McCarthy. When National Guardsmen and the Chicago police were ordered to disperse the crowd, violence erupted. In front of a battery of television cameras, hundreds of people, among them bystanders and a few reporters, were beaten with clubs. Throughout the nation, there were accusations that the police and the Guardsmen had overreacted and had used undue force in breaking up an assembly that, though noisy, was essentially peaceful.

The Fifth and Sixth Amendments

Both the Fifth and Sixth Amendments pertain to the rights of an accused person when taken into custody and brought to trial. Among those rights stated in the Fifth Amendment, one holds that the accused "shall not be compelled to be a witness against himself," meaning that everyone has the right to remain silent when asked questions that will lead to self-incriminating answers. And among those in the Sixth Amendment is the right entitling the defendant (the accused) to "the assistance of counsel [an attorney] for his defense."

Over the years, many people have accused the police of violating each of these amendments, either singly or together. A number of accusers have taken their complaints to court, with some of the cases then advancing to the U.S. Supreme Court for consideration. The amendments were linked together in two extremely important Supreme Court cases of the 1960s. The two cases illustrated the manner in which the police often violated the amendments, and the decisions reached by the Court altered significantly the way in which the police are able to deal with an accused person. They are decisions that will affect your conduct for as long as you are an officer—or until the decisions are altered by a future Supreme Court. The cases involved two young men—Danny Escobedo and Ernesto A. Miranda.

THE *ESCOBEDO* DECISION

Danny Escobedo, a Mexican-American laborer in his twenties, was arrested by Chicago police in 1960 in connection with a murder.[4] During his questioning, the police refused to allow the young man to speak with an attorney. They also failed to inform him of his constitutional right to remain silent and make no self-incriminating statements. When he later went to trial, Escobedo was found guilty and imprisoned chiefly on the answers that he gave during his police interrogation.

Escobedo's attorney objected to the verdict and took his client's case to the Supreme Court in 1964. The Court ruled that Escobedo's statements to the police could not be used to convict him. In the main, the Court based its decision on the opinion that the police had denied the young man his Sixth Amendment right to legal counsel.

The decision proved to be a troublesome one for the police to handle. The problem stemmed from the fact that the Court, in its ruling, did not set out any clear guidelines for the police to follow when dealing with accused persons in the future. What was needed were specific steps that the police could take to see that they did not, even in the smallest technical way, violate the Fifth and Sixth Amendment rights of the accused.

Two years later, in 1966, the Court's ruling in the *Miranda* case set forth the needed guidelines.

THE *MIRANDA* DECISION

In 1961, twenty-one-year-old Ernesto A. Miranda was arrested by police in Phoenix, Arizona, on suspicion of having kidnapped, raped, and robbed a high school girl.[5] (He reportedly took $4 from her.) Picked up by police because the girl managed to remember the number on his car license plate, Miranda was taken to headquarters for questioning. There, he signed a confession in which he admitted to the charges and stated that the confession was being made voluntarily and with full knowledge of his legal rights. He said he understood that any statements he made to the police and in the confession could be used against him in court.

When Miranda went to trial, his confession was introduced as evidence and led to his conviction and a prison sentence of forty to fifty-five years. (The sentence included a conviction for an $8 armed robbery in an unrelated case.) His attorney appealed the verdict to the Arizona Supreme Court. The attorney argued that the sentence should be overturned because the police, despite having Miranda sign statements concerning his legal rights, had not informed him of his Sixth Amendment right to legal counsel and had not adequately protected his Fifth Amendment right to remain silent. The Arizona Supreme Court disagreed with the argument and upheld the conviction and sentence.

The case was then appealed to the U.S. Supreme Court in 1966. There, the conviction and sentence were overturned. The Supreme Court, under Chief Justice Earl Warren, held that Miranda's Fifth and Sixth Amendment rights had, indeed, been violated. The Court then went on to set out guidelines that the police should follow to ensure that these rights were adequately protected in the future. The guidelines drastically changed the manner in which the police are able to deal with suspects during and after an arrest.

THE *MIRANDA* GUIDELINES

To see how the guidelines have changed things, let's look first at how you would have acted as an officer in the years prior to the *Miranda* decision. At that time, you held several responsibilities to persons accused of a crime. First, you were required to be certain that they made their confessions voluntarily; you could not threaten or physically beat them into an admission of guilt. Second, you were required to be reasonably sure that the confessions were trustworthy and that no suspect was one of those people who, to punish themselves or get their names in the newspapers, plague all police departments by confessing to crimes that they did not commit. (As a further safeguard here, you could not seek to get a conviction with the confession alone; you had to seek out evidence to corroborate its contents.) Finally, you were not to make any false promises to the suspects, saying, for instance, that you would see that the charges against them would be reduced if they "saved everyone a lot of time and trouble" by confessing.

As an officer working in the years since the *Miranda* decision, you hold these same responsibilities. But you are faced with some extra duties. In keeping with the Supreme Court guidelines, you must now, prior to any questioning about the crime, inform the accused person of his or her Fifth and Sixth Amendment rights. Then, once the rights have been explained, you must honor all responses to them. The rights are listed on a small card that you carry at all times, and you read them aloud when the time comes to question the accused. The card is known widely as the

---

MIRANDA WARNING

1. You have the right to remain silent.
2. Anything you say can and will be used against you in a court of law.
3. You have the right to talk to a lawyer and have him present with you while you are being questioned.
4. If you cannot afford to hire a lawyer, one will be appointed to represent you before any questioning, if you wish one.

WAIVER

After the warning and in order to secure a waiver, the following questions should be asked and an affirmative reply secured to each question:

1. Do you understand each of these rights I have explained to you ?
2. Having these rights in mind, do you wish to talk to us now ?

"Miranda card." After reading the four rights, you would read the two questions under "Waiver."

Since the material on the *Miranda* card is given orally, there is always the chance that accused persons will say they were denied their rights because the police officer forgot or deliberately failed to read them. To safeguard against this possibility, departments also use a written document that the accused signs. It usually reads as follows:

CONSTITUTIONAL RIGHTS AND WARNINGS

Date _____ Place _____ Time _____
Name _____ Date of Birth _____

1. *That I have the right to remain silent and not make any statement at all.*
   I understand this segment (initial)

   _____

2. *That anything I say can and will be used against me in a court or courts of law for the offense or offenses by which this warning is executed.*
   I understand this segment (initial)

   _____

3. *That I can hire a lawyer of my own choice to be present and advise me before and during any statement.*
   I understand this segment (initial)

   _____

4. *That if I am unable to hire a lawyer I can request and receive appointment of a lawyer by the proper authority, without any cost or charge to me.*
   I understand this segment (initial)

   _____

I have read or have had read to me the four (4) inclusive segments stipulating my Constitutional rights and understand each to the fullest extent.

_____
Signature

Witnessed:

_____

_____

Contrary to popular belief, the reading of the rights does not have to take place at the time of arrest. Though they do take place at that time on occasion, *they need not be read until you actually begin to question the person about the crime of which he or she is accused.* You are legally entitled to arrest suspects and place them in custody before informing them of their rights and beginning your interrogation.

This procedure enables an officer to better deal with angry or emotionally upset suspects. Also, in many instances, it provides time for the emotions of both the suspect and the officer to cool before questioning begins. Both parties are thus safeguarded. The officer is protected from asking questions when, in the heat of the moment, he or she may have forgotten to read the rights (that forgetfulness can see the arrest voided on the basis that the suspect's constitutional rights were violated). The suspect is protected against making on-the-spur-of-the-moment statements that could be self-damaging.

At the time of an arrest, however, you may, without reading the rights, ask questions that do not apply directly to the crime. You may, for example, ask suspects for their names, addresses, telephone numbers, and ages.

Now suppose that you come upon a crime that has just been committed or is in progress. On the basis of various court decisions over the years, you are permitted, before reading the rights, to ask suspects such questions as: "Do you want to tell me who you are and what you're doing

here? Do you want to tell me what's been happening here?"
Questions of this nature are seen as reasonable to help the
officer fashion a picture of what has been occurring. The
suspects may refuse to answer or, especially if not guilty,
may be eager to explain the situation.

THE *MIRANDA* CONTROVERSY

As soon as it took effect, the Miranda decision triggered a
widespread controversy among the public and police.[6] A
great segment of the public strongly opposed the measure
(and still does), saying that it gave a guilty person too much
of a chance to escape punishment. The slightest error on
the part of the police in carrying out the guidelines could
see the case against an obviously guilty defendant dis-
missed, with the defendant then going free. Since there
was such an opportunity to avoid punishment, the belief
here was that more and more people would be tempted to
commit crimes.

Just as great a segment of the public approved of the
Court's action—and continues to do so. The decision, its
supporters argued, insured that all persons, when caught
in the drama of an arrest and held by an organization that
they saw as hostile and frightening, would not be allowed
to forget that they hold certain inalienable constitutional
rights. In all, the feeling was that the preservation of those
rights must always outweigh the possibility that now and
again a guilty person might escape punishment.

Police opinion was just as sharply divided. Many officers said that the *Miranda* card would put an additional
burden on them when questions could not be delayed but
had to be asked at the time of an arrest, an act that is
ticklish enough under the best of circumstances. The reading of the rights could make this extra burden especially
troublesome when the officers were dealing with someone
who was angry or resisting them. They would be forced to

struggle with the card and the accused all at the same time. Other officers maintained that a person is customarily upset about being arrested. The formal reading of the rights would only heighten that upset and make the arrest all the more difficult and dangerous.

On the other hand, there were officers who felt that the *Miranda* card did not promise to be much of a problem. It would take but a few seconds to read. If the questioning and the arrest were carried out in a quiet and professional manner, the card would not necessarily cause the accused person to become unduly upset.

In the years since, the police have become accustomed to the card's use and, in the main, have not found it to be as much trouble as originally thought. Since the card needs to be read only at the time a suspect is questioned, the departments have found it wise not to begin their questioning at the moment of the arrest if at all possible. Interrogation is delayed until the accused has been taken to headquarters and tempers have had the chance to cool.

The police have also come to see that card as a protection for themselves as well as for the accused. It helps to safeguard their arrests from later being invalidated by charges that the accused person's Fifth and Sixth Amendment rights were accidentally or deliberately violated.

When the decision was first announced, there were predictions that it would enable armies of lawbreakers to go free. They would do so by simply refusing to speak or by later having the cases against them overturned by claiming that their confessions had been illegally obtained. Studies taken since then have shown the results not to be as dire as expected.

One early study dealt with the accused escaping punishment by remaining silent. Conducted in 1966 by the district attorney of Los Angeles County, it looked at some 40,000 felony cases. Revealed was the fact that only in a small percentage of the cases (less than 10 percent) had a confession been needed to bring the accused to trial. Most cases had gone to court on the basis of evidence other than confessions—evidence, for example, found at the scene of the crime or given by witnesses. The study also showed that many suspects preferred not to remain silent. They confessed despite police admonitions that they need not speak and were entitled to the help of an attorney.[7]

A year later, Ramsey Clark, U.S. attorney general at the time, spoke about the fear of the guilty going free because the cases against them were overturned by the courts. He told a congressional committee of a study made of a number of overturned cases. He said that the authorities had been able to take them back to court for retrial and that convictions had then been obtained.

(Miranda himself was retried and reconvicted in the wake of the Court's decision. He was paroled after serving five years of a twenty-year sentence. In 1976, Miranda was stabbed to death in a barroom fight over a $2 card game.)

Despite the above studies—and others like them—much opposition to the *Miranda* decision has remained through the years. Several official steps have been taken to limit its scope. For one, the Supreme Court itself, under Chief Justice Warren Burger, ruled in the 1970s that a confession obtained in violation of the *Miranda* decision can be used at a trial to prove that the defendant is lying.

For another, in 1987, U.S. Attorney General Edwin Meese urged that the wording in the *Miranda* warning be changed on the grounds that it hinders criminal investigations.[8] He and the Justice Department suggested that the warning be revised so that it (1) drops the mention of the accused's right to legal counsel, (2) mentions the accused's right to remain silent, but (3) closes with the following sentence: "Your failure to talk at this interview could make it harder for a judge or jury to believe any story you give later on."

Meese's suggestion brought a storm of protest from attorneys and organizations such as the American Civil Liberties Union. The dropping of the mention of the right to remain silent was seen as especially unfair on accused persons who, new to the country or without sufficient education, might not be fully aware of their constitutional rights. The proposed final sentence was regarded as particularly dangerous for everyone. It strongly indicated to accused persons that they might well be in deeper trouble in court if they exercised their right to remain silent. This threat could well frighten them into confessions. The authorities could then claim that the confessions had been given voluntarily when actually they had been forced from the accused through fear.

As of the writing of this book, the card had not been modified.

* * *

Quite rightfully, the public will expect you and your department always to operate according to the demands of the nation's Constitution and Bill of Rights. This is a very basic American view. But it is also just one view that our public holds on the role of the police in U.S. society. There is another widely held opinion of law enforcement and what it is supposed to do. It is a particular view with which you'll have to live as an officer and which may cause you difficulty in your work. It is the subject of the next chapter.

5

Police and Public
The Crime-Fighter Myth

What is this particular view that the public holds of the police and their work?

To see what it is, you need only ask anyone two questions: *What do the police do?* and *What are they supposed to do?* The chances are, you'll get such answers as: *They catch criminals . . . They're the law and order guys . . . They enforce the law . . . They protect us.* Or you might hear this very poetic one: *They're the "thin blue line" that guards us against crime.*

The answers all share a point in common. In mentioning such matters as "catching criminals," "enforcing the law," and being "a thin blue line," they highlight the fact that the public thinks of the police as mainly crime fighters.

This view is far from the truth, so far away that it can be called a myth. As you know, your duties as an officer involve far more than crime fighting. You're a peace-keeper and act as such every time you stop a family fight or take a lost child in hand. You're a social worker and perform as such every time you refer a troubled person to a public or private agency for help.

Certainly, as an officer, you'll often run up against criminal activities and be involved in criminal investigations. But the truth is that only a small percentage of your time will be given to these kinds of work. Later in the chapter, we'll see just how small this percentage is. Yet the overwhelming impression of you as a crime fighter remains with the public.

THE CRIME-FIGHTER MYTH

The myth likely stems from the fact that many early police officers—among them the reeves of rural England and Robert Peel's bobbies of London—were involved principally in combating criminal activities. It is a myth that, for several reasons, is especially prevalent in our day and age.

An Era of Crime

To begin, countless people today desperately *want* to look on the police as crime fighters. This is because we live in an era in which there is much crime, particularly much violent crime, and a fearful public yearns to be protected from it. For various reasons—among them mounting drug abuse, the crowded conditions in our growing cities, and the disdain for public institutions that erupted among people, especially the young, during the Vietnam conflict—the U.S. crime rate has shown a pretty steady increase over the past fifteen to twenty years. It reached its peak in 1980, lingered at about the same level in 1981, and dipped between 1982 and 1984. Despite the dip, the rate remained high. Then it began to mount again in 1985.

In 1986, the *Uniform Crime Reports for the United States*, an annual publication of the Federal Bureau of Investigation, revealed that some 12,430,000 crimes were reported in the country during 1985. They divided themselves between 1,327,400 violent crimes (murder as an example) and 11,102,600 property crimes (burglary, for example). The total crimes reported in 1984 stood at 11,881,800.[1]

The *Uniform Crime Reports* provides figures on eight types of crimes. They range from murder to robbery, burglary, and auto theft. (*Robbery* is generally defined as "the taking of someone's property by force or by creating the fear of force and violence." The general definition of *burglary* is "the unlawful entry of a structure to commit a theft or a felony.") As the figures below show, some crimes in 1985 remained down in number from that peak year of 1980. But all offenses in 1985 reached totals above those in 1984.

Here now are some of the figures[2]:

- Murder and non-negligent (meaning not accidental) manslaughter: 18,976 cases in 1985, a rise of 1.5 percent over 18,692 in 1984. (The figure is down from 1980, a year in which 23,040 cases in this category were reported.)

- Robbery: 497,874 offenses in 1985, up 2.7 percent over 485,008 the year before. (Down from 1980's total of 565,840.)

- Burglary: 3,073,348 cases in 1985, an increase of 3.0 percent over 1984's 2,984,434. (Down from 3,327,700 in 1980.)

In addition to living in an era of widespread crime, we live in a time of instant communication. Crime news comes to us from every direction and often arrives via radio and television minutes after a robbery or murder has taken place. The flood of such news greatly heightens our awareness and fear of the ugliness going on around us. It is easy to understand why a nervous public so much wants to view its police as dedicated crime fighters.

The News Media

Criminologist Samuel Walker, in his book *The Police in America: An Introduction*, speaks of the next factors that mold the public's view of the police as mainly crime fighters.[3] He begins with the problem just mentioned—today's widespread news coverage. He writes that the news media (newspapers, news magazines, and radio and television news) all place a heavy emphasis on crime in their coverage of daily events. Accounting for much of the concentration is the fact that crimes make fascinating stories that attract us all. But, in concentrating on such stories, the news media does more than simply heighten our awareness and fear of the ugliness around us. By ignoring or paying scant attention to items that concern other aspects of police work, it also gives us a false impression of what is being done by the departments.

The Entertainment Industry

Walker then turns to the part played by the entertainment industry. Here, he focuses on television's many cop shows. He writes that he understands why such shows are so popular. By its very nature, a crime story contains all the basic elements for a rousing yarn. There is a clearly defined hero and a clearly defined villain. There is plenty of room for action. And all the room in the world for an exciting conclusion when the "bad guys" are finally brought to justice.

Though there are occasional exceptions, Walker goes on to say that the cop shows give a false impression of police work by concentrating on crime plots to take advantage of all the action. They leave the public with the idea that the police do little else but fight crime. And they give a mistaken idea of how the police actually do deal with crime and criminals.

To prove this last point, Walker cites two studies made in the 1970s. The first looked at how fifteen prime-time shows dealt with the police handling of constitutional rights. As was said in Chapter Four, officers are required to protect the constitutional rights of every suspect and know that they risk having cases overturned if they fail—even accidentally—to do so. Yet the study revealed that the fifteen shows had scenes containing twenty-one police violations of constitutional rights, seven failures to mention those rights to a suspect, and fifteen instances of police brutality and harassment.

The next study looked at how the cop shows have given an inaccurate picture of police investigations. Chief among its points (which can also be applied to the motion picture produced for theater showings) were the following two, which accused the programs of:

- Placing an overemphasis on violence and action in solving crimes.

- Placing an overemphasis on sophisticated technical methods and gear in solving crimes.

TRUTH VERSUS MYTH

If the public's view of the police as mainly crime fighters is a myth, then what is the truth of the matter?

To begin, as said earlier, you'll give only a small share of your time to crime investigations once you go on duty. Just how small a share? In *The Police in America*, Samuel Walker points to several researches that provide the answer. Some reveal that officers typically devote about 20 percent of their time to activities relating to law enforcement. Others set the amount of time as low as 10 percent.[4] Hence, between 80 and 90 percent of your work will be given to your peace-keeping and referral duties, plus your training and such chores as writing reports on your day's cases.

Next, consider the contrasts between the television "cop" shows and reality.

As we know from the daily news, there is no doubt that the police can at times be as guilty of violent behavior as the TV "cops." This behavior is caused by several factors. They include an individual officer's bullying or unstable nature, the fears triggered by enraged or vicious suspects, and the anger and frustrations felt when dealing with resisting and taunting suspects. The types of violent behavior seen in officers and the factors responsible for them will be discussed more fully in Chapter Eight.

Though violence is known to be a reality of police work, no one can say exactly how many or how few incidents of violent officer conduct occur annually. There are no complete and reliable statistics on the matter. The rate may be high; it may be low. Some slight indication of what it might actually be was seen in studies made in the late 1960s for the President's Commission on Law Enforcement. They showed that in 3,826 cases the police used what was termed "undue force" in thirty-seven instances. But did those thirty-seven instances indicate a high or low incidence of excessive force? The answer depended on an individual's views. Some people argued that it was high and that "undue force" should *never* be present in police work. Others felt that, since the use of force is often necessary in the work, a few instances of its "undue" application are to be expected.[5]

But, whether the incidence is high or low, is there as much violence in actual policing as is depicted on television? The answer seems to be a definite no because of the many safeguards against such conduct that are built into today's police work. For example:

A department's preemployment background checks and psychological examinations are in great part aimed at weeding out those bullying and unstable personalities that promise behavior from the officious to the outright brutal. Academy physical training puts the emphasis on defensive rather than offensive fighting skills. Weapons training stresses firing a gun as the last resort to protect yourself, a fellow officer, or the public. Further, most departments maintain *internal affairs* units for investigating alleged officer misdeeds; proof of an officer's guilt can lead to dismissal from the force. These varied safeguards are designed to meet the long-standing legal requirement that officers respond to force with the least amount of force possible, just enough to solve the problem and end the threat to their persons. (This rule, remember, also applies to all citizens.)

Further, today's policemen and policewomen are urged to live up to the image of the "professional officer," an officer whose conduct is always courteous and controlled. The image is fostered by the departments in their academy and on-the-job training and by various police organizations (such as the California Peace Officers Association and the Peace Officers Research Association) in their literature and educational programs. The Law Enforcement Code of Ethics (cited in Chapter Two) is an expression of the behavior and attitudes embraced by the professional officer.

Granted, some bad apples do slip past the preemployment checks and tests. Granted, some officers do give in to the factors that can produce violence in them. And, granted, officer misconduct is a fact of police life to one degree or another. But the deterrents to violence are many today. In the eyes of some observers—among them the authors of *Participants in American Criminal Justice: The Promise and the Performance*—they have reduced the incidence of police brutality over the past years. And they have certainly made the idea that the undisciplined behavior seen in some TV cops is commonplace and condoned seem silly.

Television Action Versus Reality

While patrolling in their cars, TV cops never go long without running into plenty of action. They're always receiving radio reports of crimes in progress, after which, with dome light flashing and siren howling, they go speeding to the scene. On arrival, they pursue the culprit in a tire-screeching race that ends in a spectacular crash or a daring maneuver that brings the escapee to a skidding halt. Or, if the culprit is on foot, they'll chase him (or her) along the sidewalk and either tackle him or pull him down from an alley wall.

There is a degree of truth in these stories. Occasionally, we come upon press reports of the police arriving on the scene in time to capture a robber or burglar. Occasionally, there are stories of high-speed police chases along a street or freeway. But the key word here is *occasionally*. On two counts, the reality of daily police work is quite different.

First, as an officer, only rarely will you come upon a crime in progress while patrolling your beat in a car or on foot. Criminals work unobtrusively, as safely out of your sight as possible. If you happen to cruise past at the moment someone is planning to enter a store to rob it, you may rest assured that he'll delay his entry until you've faded from view. Also, criminals work quickly, taking only a few seconds or, at most, a few minutes to get the job done. You can be cruising along a street at the moment a mugging is taking place just around the corner. By the time you turn that corner, the culprit will likely have vanished.

Second, only rarely will you receive a radio call of a crime in progress. In the vast majority of cases, the victims take no action at the scene. To use a store robbery as an example, some are too frightened to move or are given no chance to steal away and telephone for help or even trigger a close-by silent alarm (an alarm that does not go off at the scene but is connected to the police department and is heard there). Moreover, virtually all companies today insist that their employees never attempt any dangerous heroics. Of even greater consequence, the victims in all types of crime usually do not summon the police until twenty minutes to an hour after the offense has been committed. This all-important time is lost while they calm themselves and try to think clearly again.

All these facts reduce, in real life, the efficient part played by the central figure in television action—the speeding patrol car.[6] Despite its speed, the cruiser's effectiveness is severely hampered by two hard facts. There is, first, that long wait on the part of the victims before summoning your help. What good is a fast-moving vehicle if the crime is an hour old and the culprit long gone?

The second fact has to do with coming upon a crime in progress. Police officials admit that the business of patrolling a beat in a car (or on foot) is a haphazard one. Sitting behind the wheel, you are not a fortune-teller with a crystal ball and so can have no idea of where trouble is about to break out. With luck, you may accidentally stumble upon an offense as it is occurring. Otherwise, you may well be at one end of your beat when a crime is committed at the other end. Only when the department receives advance word that there is something in the wind do you have any real chance of being in the right place at the right time.

Then what is the value of the patrolling cruiser? When it first came into wide use in the 1920s, the departments thought that, because of its speed, the car could do a better job of apprehending criminals and getting to emergencies than could the officer of that day—the patrolman on foot. Since then, it has proved to be of mixed value. On the one hand, as was said a moment ago, what is the good of all that speed when victims wait so long before summoning you? On the other hand, one of your principal duties while on patrol will be to watch for persons and motor vehicles on the department's "wanted" list. Should the driver of, say, a stolen car take flight on being sighted, you'll be able to pursue when a chase on foot would be out of the question.

The departments also thought that the car, with its ability to cover a beat more quickly than the officer on foot, would give the police a greater public visibility. In turn,

Police patrolling neighborhood in cruiser

so the departments believed, this would tend to deter the committing of crimes and would instill in the public a greater sense of safety. Both beliefs are being seriously questioned at present. Some police officials say that the car has been of limited help in both cases. Others, pointing to the rising crime rate, argue that it has had no effect on the number of offenses committed or on the public's feelings of safety. There are no unarguable statistics to prove the matter one way or the other—only questions and concerns.

One great concern about the car has to do with a problem that we'll explain and talk about later in this chapter— the chasm of dislike and distrust that has been forged over the years between the police and great segments of the public. The car is said to be much responsible for this chasm. The departments, by removing their officers from the sidewalk and placing them in steel capsules, have greatly reduced the opportunity for the officers to become friends with the people on their beats. No longer do they have, at any moment, the chance to stop and chat with neighbors and local business people. To do so, they must deliberately stop and climb out from behind the wheel. In the minds of many people, the cruiser has not only helped to turn officers into distant, alien figures but has also left the sidewalks more open to the criminal than ever before.

Television Investigations Versus Reality

Now, what of that investigative equipment that plays such a role in solving television cases? In real life, it is often damaged by the delays in reporting crimes. Twenty to sixty minutes provides ample time for incriminating fingerprints to be smeared or obliterated by victims and witnesses. Ample time for the people on the scene to tamper thoughtlessly with other types of evidence, perhaps by sweeping away bits of broken glass with shreds of the culprit's clothing or splashes of his (or her) blood clinging to them. And ample time for everyone to begin forgetting vital details about the culprit—physical details that would insure an accurate composite drawing of his features by a police artist or behavioral details that the police could then check against the records of the operational methods of known criminals.

Regardless of what happens on television, you'll find that, while such investigative tools as fingerprints, voice prints, polygraphs, composite drawings, and ballistic examinations of weapons are helpful and at times crucial, the success of your criminal investigations will usually hinge on other factors. Chief among them are confessions by suspects, reports by reliable witnesses, and, perhaps most important of all, material gathered from the many sources of information on your beat. Luck will sometimes play a part. At times, a thief will accidentally leave his wallet—complete with driver's license inside—or some other identifying possession at the scene.

And, at times, it will seem as if the culprit, suffering pangs of conscience, is trying to help you catch him. A case in point here is the burglar who was standing on lookout in an office while his cohort broke into a safe in an adjoining room. He was attracted to a new typewriter on a desk and, to pass the time, sat down and began to experiment with it, pecking out his name in the process— and then forgetting to remove the sheet of paper when he and his partner departed. Was his oversight an accident or a secret desire to be caught? Who can tell?

Now let's talk for a moment about the sources of information on your beat.[7] These are the bartenders, hotel clerks and bellhops, newspaper dealers, barbers, merchants, gossipy residents, and young people whom you see daily while on patrol. Officers know that one of their most important duties is to climb out of their cars and get to know these people on friendly terms. Their friendship can pay great dividends in a department's crime-fighting and crime-prevention work. Many hate the crime in their neighborhood and, on getting to like and trust you, will quickly report offenses or signs of coming trouble; some will even be willing to serve later as witnesses in court. Many others have contacts with criminals or criminal networks. When time is taken to cultivate a relationship with them and to learn the right questions to ask, these sources can provide an officer with valuable information on what trouble is happening or about to happen—about to "go down"—in the neighborhood.

One of your most valuable sources will be the neighborhood people on the fringes of crime. On cultivating them, you'll find that many are willing to be informants for a few dollars or a favor now and again. Once called by such names as *stool pigeons*, *stoolies*, and *canaries*, they're now usually known as *snitches*. An ugly but necessary part of your role in society is to get to know and use them.

Criminal investigations are always interesting and exciting, but they customarily bear little semblance to the derring-do, high-speed, plenty-of-gunfire operations seen on television and motion-picture screens. Rather, they involve a patient routine of asking questions and tracking down information that it is hoped will lead to an arrest. And, for both plainclothes detectives and uniformed patrol officers, investigations differ from their TV and film counterparts in yet another way. On the screen, the detectives usually concentrate on just one case per episode. In real life, detectives handle a number of cases simultaneously and must give attention to them all. In real life, your investigations as a uniformed officer are constantly interrupted by those peace-keeping and referral calls that take up the major share of your duty hours.[8]

This last point brings us to an amazing gap in the public's thinking. People will call you twenty-four hours a day for help in every noncrime matter imaginable—from bothersome yapping dogs to family squabbles. They'll expect you to do anything from lecture misbehaving children to give medical help in emergencies—or know where to get it quickly. They'll expect you to know the public and private agencies to which they can turn for help. Yet, in light of all this, many members of the public will persistently overlook the fact that you are a peace-keeper and social worker and insist on thinking of you mainly as a crime fighter. It's a strange phenomenon.

THE MYTH AND ITS DAMAGE

The myth of the crime fighter has long done the police damage. The damage is particularly great in our era, with all its crime and violence. People are alarmed at what is happening and ask, *Why don't the police put a stop to it?* And then, seeing the generally rising crime rate of the past fifteen to twenty years, they answer their own question: *The police are failing in their duty to us.*

This answer, true or not, has led to a widespread public contempt for the police and has jeopardized their role in our society.

Are the Police Failing?

But is it a just and fair answer? To see, we need to look at what is called the *crime clearance rate.* The rate, as defined by the Federal Bureau of Investigation, refers to the number of cases the police clear up by identifying an offender, finding sufficient evidence to charge him, and actually taking him into custody. In all, it indicates how well or how poorly the police are doing in solving cases.[9]

Also included in the rate are those instances when the police have the necessary identification and evidence but are unable to make an arrest for some reason beyond their control. Obvious examples here would be the death of the offender or his escape from the country before he came under suspicion.

In the 1986 issue of *Uniform Crime Reports,* the Federal Bureau of Investigation gives a mixed picture of police success in clearing cases during 1985.[10] They did well that year in some crime areas and had difficulty with others. As had been true in other years, their success hinged principally on the identification of offenders and was understandably at its greatest in cases where the culprit was seen by helpful witnesses or victims.

Murder, which so often occurs in the midst of family fights, had the highest clearance rate for the year—72 percent. Fifty-four percent of the forcible rape cases were cleared. The rate for robbery stood much lower, at 25 percent—in great part because many victims are so rattled that they are unable to provide helpful descriptions.

The rates were lowest in the so-called sneaky crimes, such as burglary and motor-vehicle theft, where the culprit is rarely seen. In 1985, the clearance rate for burglary was 14 percent, and for vehicle theft, 15 percent.

The *Uniform Crime Reports* gives not only a mixed but also an incomplete picture of police success or failure because it is able to cover only reported crimes. Estimates hold that no more than 50 percent of some offenses, robbery among them, are ever reported to the police. Were *all* offenses reported, the police might earn better—or worse—clearance rates. Until that happens, it is difficult to judge whether the police are doing a good or a poor job.

Hurting Themselves

Many officers have allowed the myth to damage themselves. Injured are those who, like the public, regard the police as principally crime fighters. In the main, the harm stems from the tendency of these officers to look on "non-crime" work—all their peace-keeping and referral duties—as not being "real" police work.[11] They are impatient with these duties and thus risk handling them with a gruffness and carelessness that ends with the work being done poorly. Understandably, the people they have served are left with angry memories and a scorn not just for the uncaring officer but for all officers.

Adding to the problem is an opinion that many officers have of the public. Called constantly to handle crime and dealing again and again with some of the world's worst people—derelicts, personalities unable to settle emotional upheavals with anything but their fists or a gun, alcoholics, drug addicts, and prostitutes, to name just a few—they soon begin thinking that everyone is "bad" and out to make trouble.

One policeman has spoken bluntly on this point. He has said that the police daily deal with "the scum" of the world. It becomes easy for officers to think the whole world is "scum."[12]

Such thinking, when reflected in an officer's cold face and bearing, cannot help but anger and alienate the public.

A GAPING CHASM

The crime-fighter myth has been much responsible for an unfortunate and dangerous situation that is widely seen today. It has helped to create a gaping chasm of mistrust and dislike between the police and great segments of the public.

Both sides must share in the blame for the chasm. Much of the public, in thinking of the police as mainly crime fighters, has misunderstood or has not learned about the total law enforcement mission. While the police have been accused of failing to reduce or eradicate the crime and violence that surround us, there has been a widespread tendency to forget the many peace-keeping and referral duties with which they are charged and which consume so much of their time.

On the opposite side of the chasm, the police are painfully aware of the public's view of them as inept crime fighters. This awareness has caused many officers to adopt an attitude that has not only helped to form the original gulf but has widened it over the years as well. Frustrated at being called failures, often themselves not understanding or liking their greater role as peace-keepers and social workers, they have retreated to an unhappy stance. They have become the "professional officer"—not the professional officer mentioned earlier, but the professional officer in the worst sense of the term: cold rather than calm, aloof rather than courteous, hard throughout. They have assumed the image of the hard-faced, helmeted, booted cop with mirror sunglasses—a distant and unfeeling figure that the public cannot help but fear and dislike.

* * *

The crime-fighter myth has done great damage. But, while it has been much responsible for opening the chasm, it has not been the only force at work here. Other factors have also played a part in deepening and widening the chasm, among them the already mentioned police car and the public complaints that were discussed in earlier chapters. These factors—and how the police are trying to correct them—are to be the subjects of our next chapters.

6

Police and Public
The Chasm Widens

Let's again pretend that you are an officer. Your department, as has been stressed before in this book, is manned by human beings with all the frailties that human beings can have. Some of your fellow officers are good cops— honest, dedicated to doing the best job possible, and thoughtful and compassionate in their dealings with the public. Some are good cops who, perhaps because of tiredness or some personal problem, fail in their duties at times or repeatedly. Others are outright bad apples who managed to get past the department's selection and training programs. They may be dishonest; they may be bullies; they may be prejudiced against many of the people with whom they must deal; they may be all of these things. Still others started out as good cops who, for one reason or another, turned rotten.

No one can say for certain how many bad apples are in police work—or how many good officers have gone sour with the passing years. As we'll see later in the chapter, periodic headlines of police scandals indicate that some departments have a great many; the New York City de-

SPOILS THE WHOLE BARREL

partment is among those accused of suffering more than their fair share (though it must be remembered that there are no statistics to show definitely how many of the city's 25,000-officer force are on the bad side.) Others, among them the Los Angeles department, are said to be troubled by but a few, and some departments by none at all. Regardless of their number, the bad cops and the good ones who turn sour have all contributed to widening the police–public chasm of dislike and distrust. They have been responsible for four types of officer misconduct—bullying, brutality, harassment,[1] and corruption.

These problem behaviors are to be the subjects of this chapter. We'll describe each in turn and then discuss why they are ugly realities in police work.

They are to be joined by a fifth problem that involves both good officers and bad apples. It is known as the police code of silence.

BULLYING

"Bullying" means that you assume an intimidating attitude or take some action that frightens or promises harm to the person with whom you're dealing. The range of such actions is wide. It includes pulling someone roughly from a car when the individual is not resisting you; glaring menacingly at a person, and drawing your sidearm when there is no need to do so.

You'll recall that, as an officer, you are allowed by law to use force, but are limited to using only a minimum of force—no more than the amount necessary to resolve the situation in which you are involved. Bullying acts, such as those above, entail or threaten to entail more than the minimal amount of force permitted by the law.

BRUTALITY

"Brutality" can be defined as the use of some type of excessive force. A case meeting this definition was reported in Queens, New York, recently. An eighteen-year-old man was picked up by six officers for allegedly selling $10 worth of marijuana. They took him to their precinct station and repeatedly gave him burning shocks with a "stun gun" (a small weapon that imparts a nonlethal electric shock) to make him confess. He was left with forty burn marks on his body.[2]

At the time this book is being written, an Oakland, California, officer is under investigation for three alleged instances of brutality. He is, first, accused of hitting a suspect with his gun and then bouncing the man's head against a concrete wall. The second charge holds that he handcuffed another suspect too tightly and slammed his face into the side of the officer's cruiser. Finally, still another suspect has accused the officer of grabbing him from behind in a choke hold and throwing him to the ground.[3]

Brutality is a frequently heard charge in cases of officer misconduct. But, while the above examples all involve unmistakable acts of brutal force, the subject is a difficult one to discuss. There are two reasons for saying this. First, despite the above examples, there is no way of knowing exactly how much brutality actually occurs in police work. The police argue that strong force is needed in many arrests, especially in those dealing with violent or strongly resisting suspects; that force may look like brutality but is really a necessary and legal action in such cases. There are no solid statistics one way or another to indicate exactly how much brutality is to be found in law enforcement.

Second, the police also argue that the question of what actually constitutes brutality is often a matter of personal opinion. They contend that some people look on any officer officiousness or coldness as bullying or even brutality while others do not. Some consider harassment a brutality; others do not. And some regard any incident in which they are stopped by the police to be a form of bullying, brutality, or harassment.[4]

The experiences of a California traffic officer lends credence to the above views. He says, "I can't tell you the number of times I've had drivers with liquor on their breath accuse me of picking on them because I've had to make them get out of the car for a breatholizer test. And, believe me, I've been damned polite with them. And I can't tell you how often my friends have walked up to a car they've pulled over and heard the driver tell his girlfriend, 'Well, here's the fuzz hassling me again.' These sorts of things just go with the job.''[5]

HARASSMENT

"Harassment" is defined as the tendency to stop, question, search, and arrest certain types of people more often than others while on patrol.

Stopping, questioning, and searching a person are the basic parts of what is called a *field interrogation*. A field interrogation is a perfectly legal police tactic. By allowing officers to stop and check on suspicious-looking people, it is designed to help maintain the peace and prevent crime. But when harassment plays a part in it—when it is directed against one type of person more than another—it breaks the nation's laws against discrimination and violates our civil rights. People are stopped not because they are actually looking or acting suspicious but because, due to some personal prejudice, an officer simply does not like their clothing, their hair style, or the color of their skin. Especially endangered here are the rights granted us under the Fourth Amendment in the Bill of Rights. That Amendment makes us safe from illegal searches and seizures (arrests)—namely searches and seizures that are carried out without adequate reason.

The field interrogation is a tactic that a late 1960s study by a special federal group, called the President's Commission on Law Enforcement, found to be universally detested by the minorities. They charged that they were the victims of far too many such interrogations; they felt they were the subjects of racial discrimination and were being deprived of their civil rights.

99

"You're a disgrace to the California state police, Stinkley! Your tie is spotted and your shoes are scuffed."

Theirs was a complaint that has been voiced for many years. It was heard in the late nineteenth and early twentieth centuries when, as police history shows, the municipal police in many cities were famous for being especially hard on the minorities. It was heard again in the 1950s and 1960s when such groups as the National Association for the Advancement of Colored People and the American Civil Liberties Union charged that the police were constantly depriving the blacks and other minorities of their civil rights by stopping, questioning, searching, and arresting them without good reason and far more often than whites.[6]

A number of comments and studies over the years substantiated these claims. In the 1950s, Judge Daniel W. Williams of southern California said that the Los Angeles police made approximately 90 percent of their arrests for gambling in black neighborhoods when the blacks made up only 10 percent of the local population and their neighborhoods were responsible for but a small fraction of the gambling activities in the city. A decade later, a northern California study claimed that the San Francisco police often harassed black teenagers and, if the youngsters protested at being questioned, often took them into custody for disorderly conduct; other studies revealed that the same thing happened in other cities across the country.[7] A later study by the San Diego, California, Police Department found that 66 percent of the field interrogations reviewed in the study were made of blacks and Mexican Americans.

But members of minority groups are not the only ones to complain of being harassed. The same charge can be made by homosexual men and women, by teenagers, and even by males as a group. The San Diego study showed that 100 percent of the subjects interrogated in the field were male. Almost two-thirds were juveniles.

There is a type of field interrogation that has antagonized people from all walks of life. It consists of what are seen as indiscriminate stops for questioning and is widely called *planned harassment*. It occurs routinely in many wealthy neighborhoods when the police stop and question any pedestrian or parked driver unfamiliar to them—even the most innocent of visitors or tourists—on the grounds that the stranger may be looking the neighborhood over for a burglary or some other offense. It also occurs when the residents of a poor or slum district demand that something be done about the crime in their neighborhood; it sees even the most innocent of pedestrians or street-corner groups questioned. In both instances, many of the people who are stopped feel that they are being subjected to questioning for no good reason and are suffering a violation of their right to use the public streets in a peaceable and law-abiding manner.

Though widely condemned as a deliberate harassment, this type of field interrogation is defended by the police. They argue that they are responding to the wishes of residents—the taxpayers who pay for police services—to be protected against potential trouble.[8]

WHY THESE PROBLEMS?

The reasons for police bullying, brutality, and harassment are many. They are presented here not to justify acts that, as in the case of the young man left with forty burn marks on his body, are unpardonable. The purpose is to help us understand why these and other actions that have earned much public criticism do take place.

Bullying and Brutality

We must begin with a repeat of the fact that, despite the best selection and training procedures, many bad apples manage to enter police work and that many good beginning officers turn bad in time. There are those officers who, as adults, are the same bullies they were as schoolchildren. There are those who, secretly harboring a low opinion of themselves, think that their uniform and sidearm turn them into tough authority figures and act accordingly. And there are those whose personalities make them unable to control their tempers when faced with one problem after another in the course of a day's work.

Next, there is the fact that the police are called constantly to scenes of trouble and deal repeatedly with some of the world's sorriest people—derelicts, alcoholics, and drug addicts among them. As a result, all officers risk falling into the trap of thinking everyone is "bad" and out to cause trouble. Those who do stumble into the trap begin to see everyone as scum. They are soon behaving as if the public will not respond to anything but a bullying or brutal force.

Further, in dealing with the seamy side of life, the police are often pitted against angry and defiant people who spit the words "pig" and "fascist" in their faces. The inevitable result is that some, despite all their training, lose their tempers and take revenge in anything from officious to outright brutal actions. As one officer has put it, "You get hit often enough with a lot of lip and you want to hit back. Maybe it's not right, but that's the way things are."[9]

Many people believe—and many officers agree with them—that the police uniform itself is responsible for some degree of the problems here. It may urge some officers to officious and bullying ways or give the impression that the officers are bullying types. Seen as especially at fault is the style of uniform that features black boots, black leather jacket, helmet, and mirror sunglasses. At the least, it makes the wearer look cold, aloof, and tough. At the worst, it makes the officer "feel tough," with the result that the officer becomes a swaggering and threatening figure.[10]

Finally, the stresses of police work are thought to be behind much bullying and brutality. These stresses are many; they include the dangers of the job, the constant dealing with trouble, the personal worries that go hand-in-hand with a modestly paying job, and the awareness that great segments of the public hate the police or scorn them

103

as failed crime fighters. In time, such pressures can prove too much for an officer and trigger behaviors previously never dreamed of. One police wife recently drove this point home when she said that her husband's work took a happy, kind, and outgoing man and transformed him into a suspicious, pessimistic, and secretive individual. He became anything but the man she had married.[11]

Added to the stresses is physical exhaustion. It can be a particular problem during the first years of police service. New officers are usually placed on night shifts. Interfering with the family's evening life and leaving an officer extremely tired, the shifts can greatly harm his or her relationships at home.

The personal problems triggered by the stresses are as many as the stresses themselves. John G. Stratton, the director of Psychological Services for the Los Angeles County Sheriff's Department, writes of these problems in his book *Police Passages*. Stratton remarks that officers may be normal, healthy individuals at the start of their careers, but that studies show them to be below par in physical and emotional health when they leave. He adds that they are also below average in longevity (length of life) and have high suicide and divorce rates. The incidence of heart attacks is also high among officers. Eighty-five percent of officer heart attacks are believed caused by stress.[12]

Obviously, much police violence can be traced to the stresses. In many otherwise friendly officers, the violence can be seen as a way they employ to "let off steam" and ease the frustrations and angers engendered by the job. Also, a number of police officials believe that many officers, especially the beginners, are guilty of misconduct because they are afraid of the dangers that can crop up at any moment on the street.

*Police uniforms and equipment
can be intimidating.*

Among the officials holding this view is Norman Stamper, the designer of a program meant to bring the police of San Diego closer to the people they serve. (The program will be described in Chapter Seven.) He has remarked that fear is often behind physical abuses, overreactions to threatening situations, and other troublesome excesses in behavior.[13] A retired police sergeant who spent his career with a big-city department, agrees. He claims that 85 percent of police officers are "afraid of the streets." Calling police work a "contact sport," he contends that the officers who mistreat suspects at the station house are the most fearful ones of all and turn to brutality as a means of relieving their anxieties.[14]

Harassment

With males, juveniles, and members of minority groups being the chief subjects of field interrogations, there is no doubt that prejudice—racial or otherwise—is at work here. If proof is needed of its presence, that proof is to be had in a number of studies. For one, a study made some years ago of the Boston, Chicago, and Washington departments revealed that about three out of every four police officers were personally prejudiced against blacks. Other researches showed that Los Angeles and New York City officers felt a deep prejudice toward Mexicans and Puerto Ricans respectively.

It is interesting to note that each of these prejudices was directed against an exceedingly large minority in the cities being studied. At the time, Boston, Chicago, and Washington all had—and still have—heavy black populations. New York City has a large Puerto Rican population, while Los Angeles has long been home for many Hispanic people. The question arises, Did the officers start out being prejudiced or did they become prejudiced after donning a badge?

106

The police are sometimes accused of harassing members of minority groups.

Several officers who were interviewed for this book felt that there was truth in both possibilities.[15] One admitted to not liking blacks ever since boyhood. Another said, "I didn't have any feelings one way or another about Mexicans until I joined the L.A. department. But cops talk a lot of shop. Some old-timer was always coming up to my locker and warning me about the trouble I could expect from the 'Mexes.' He was just trying to help, trying to teach me the ropes, but after a while, I began to think they were creeps and got real leery whenever I had to deal with one."

These officers are not the only ones to admit to prejudice in police ranks. Representative of what many officers have to say of themselves is this statement from a West Coast patrolman. "I was teamed as partners with one guy for eight years. If there was anything he hated, it was homosexuals. Just let him see someone who looked like a gay while we were cruising around and he'd start to grin right away and say something like, 'There's another one of them creeps. Let's go.' And out I'd have to get with him and stand around while he questioned this poor guy and treated him like he was vermin. It was embarrassing."

Why didn't the officer do something to correct the situation? "What could I do? I tried to talk him out of some stops, but he wouldn't listen. It was causing bad blood between us, and that's something you don't want when you have to work eight hours a day with a guy. And I didn't want to complain about him to the precinct captain and get him into trouble. After all, he *was* my partner."

Though overt prejudice of one sort or another plays a major role in harassment, is it *always* at fault? One police expert, California criminology professor Jerome Skolnick, thinks not. Skolnick, the author of *The Police and the Urban Ghetto*, believes that something quite different might be at work in many field interrogations. He argues that officers often develop the habit of thinking of people in terms of stereotypes, meaning that they ascribe certain characteristics to what seem to be certain types of people. For example, if they've had trouble with teenage male delinquents who have long hair, wear dirty clothing, and face the world with profanity and sullen expressions, they soon develop the idea that anyone matching this description is a potential troublemaker and should be stopped for questioning. It is a sort of mental "shorthand" that—though often far from reliable—enables the police to work more quickly.[16]

Skolnick then brings up another point. He states that officers may be searching for a robbery suspect who is described only as a black male. Consequently, a great many black males in a ghetto area with a high crime rate will be stopped for questioning. This occurs, Skolnick says, not because of racial prejudice but because the men match the suspect's general description. Their appearance—their clothing and such—also likely fits the stereotype image that the officers have developed of black offenders over the years.[17]

CORRUPTION

For many officers, their contacts with the underworld lead to the desire to get in on the "easy money" that the criminal seems to make.[18] This desire has resulted in a number of shocking news stories over the years. In Key West, Florida, recently, a deputy chief of police and two detectives were convicted of running a protection racket for drug smugglers. To the north, in Chattanooga, Tennessee, a narcotics detective was charged with selling information about department drug investigations to a major cocaine-distribution ring. Still farther north, a federal court found ten Chicago policemen guilty of taking payoffs to protect two around-the-clock heroin street markets; six of the group were sentenced to twenty years each, while four received ten-year sentences.

Police corruption is defined as "the misuse of authority

by a police officer in a manner designed to produce personal gain for the officer or for others." It is a terrible fact of police life, and because it can take so many forms, it is thought to be widespread. It is also a very old problem. Police experts, among them Lawrence Sherman, the editor of *Police Corruption: A Sociological Perspective*, say that it has been present in police work for as long as there has been police work.

It is present because, as an officer, you are a protector. Many people are willing to pay you for favors ranging from giving them an extra bit of protection to participating with them in their criminal activities. It threatens you from your first day on the job. Should you ever give in to its temptations, you'll find that it usually follows a set course.

The trouble starts when you accept what seem to be innocent gifts from the business people on your beat—a free cup of coffee or a free meal. It worsens when the gifts become money—a few dollars, say, for allowing a bar to stay open for an hour or so after the legal closing time.

Next, you graduate to taking $5 or $10 from a speeding motorist to forget the traffic citation you planned to write. By this time, you're also accepting a few dollars from merchants to overlook safety violations in their places of business. And you're accepting gifts—perhaps money or a case of canned goods—from taxi and truck drivers to allow them to park in no-parking zones.

By now, accustomed to corruption in its minor forms, you're ready for something bigger. The criminals and various shady types on your beat have come to know that you can be "had." To keep you from bothering them, the gamblers will begin to cut you in on a share of their profits. Prostitutes and their pimps will pay you to "look the other way" when they're around. Drug dealers will do the same and often, as happened in the example cases that opened this section, draw you into their business, paying you well for such services as providing them with armed protection against rival dealers, informing them of planned department "busts," and bringing them new customers.

On top of all else, you've come so far that you may be engaged in a criminal business of your own, perhaps peddling drugs on your own, perhaps committing burglaries.

But these are not the only forms of corruption. You will be termed corrupt if you learn to use a drug while on patrol and then make your purchases from your dealer friends on the street. Or suppose the department charges that you are not doing enough to stop the crime around you. And so, to make an arrest, you then buy or steal some marijuana and use it to bribe one of your snitches into telling you about a crime being planned. You may end up putting a stop to that crime, but you're still guilty of a form of corruption because you broke the law—used an illegal drug—to gain your information.[19]

As is true of bullying and brutality, no one knows the full extent of corruption in police work. What can be said is that, while corruption seems to be widespread, nowhere near *all* officers succumb to it. The truth is that it is a problem only for some departments and no problem at all for others. As the authors of *Participants in Criminal Justice* point out, much of the evidence that the public has of corruption comes from such cities as New York, Philadelphia, and Chicago. There, over the years, the press has periodically carried reports of corrupt acts by some officers and their superiors. In other cities—among them Kansas City, Missouri, and Los Angeles—corruption seems nonexistent. Some of these latter cities were once plagued with the problem but have cleared it away with careful personnel selection and training measures.[20]

THE CODE OF SILENCE

The code of silence is a code of protection that has done great harm to officers and departments alike over the years. We saw an example of it a few pages ago when the West Coast officer refused to turn his partner in to the precinct captain for harassing homosexuals. Another example is provided by the recent case of a New York City policeman. During his off-duty hours, he and a woman friend got into an argument while at dinner at a restaurant. When the woman became enraged, the officer picked her up and began to carry her toward the front door, at which time the proprietor rushed to her aid. According to the surrounding diners, the officer struck the proprietor with a pistol, handcuffed him, threw him to the floor, and then kicked him in the face. A restaurant employee also tried to intervene, only to be punched in the face and handcuffed. The officer then threatened to shoot the people who had gathered round.

Police were summoned and put an end to the incident, after which the case was investigated by the department. Many civilian witnesses stepped forward to testify against the officer in the course of the investigation. But, though his actions were obviously beyond reason, not one of the officers called to the scene would speak up. They refused to comment on what they had seen of their fellow officer's behavior. In fact, they refused to discuss all aspects of the incident. Their protective silence disgusted the press and the public.[21]

In another case, a patrol car slammed into two pedestrians, killing one and injuring the other. Defying the law that requires drivers in an accident to remain at the scene, the sergeant at the wheel drove off. There were two officers with him. Not one of the three reported the accident. Later, when witnesses brought the case to the attention of the chief of police, the department officers proved loath to help with the investigation that followed.[22]

Why the Code?

In the public view, it is nothing short of reprehensible for officers to protect a fellow officer who is guilty of misconduct. The police are guardians of the law and are sworn

113

to protect the rights of all citizens. Consequently, their silence when faced by misconduct or corruption within their ranks is seen as not only dangerous but also as completely at odds with the ethics of their occupation.

This being the case, why do they protect guilty co-workers? The reasons are several. For one, they are loyal to each other as fellow officers; none of them wants to betray that loyalty by snitching. For another, like countless other people, they have been taught from childhood that it is wrong to "tell on someone." It's a lesson that, for many policemen and women, never goes away.

For still another, as an officer told the writers of this book, "We deal with all kinds of people. Sometimes we deal with law-abiding citizens. Sometimes with criminal elements. There are a lot of people on both sides who either dislike us or distrust us. And a lot who don't respect us because they don't think we do a good job. Or know that we don't make a lot of money. This makes you feel like a stranger in both camps." As strangers in "both camps"— in both the criminal and law-abiding worlds—many officers see themselves as isolated among their own kind and then feel compelled to protect "their own" with their silence.[23]

* * *

The departments are aware of the many problems that have widened the chasm of police-public misunderstanding. The past years have seen them take a number of steps in an effort to correct the problems and close the chasm. What they have done—and are doing—is the subject of the next chapter.

7

Police and Public
Working to Close the Chasm

Just as they are aware of the chasm, so are the departments
aware of the forces that can lead to officer misconduct and
corruption. And they are acutely aware that the misbehavior of even one officer can give an entire department a bad
name and damage the work and reputations of their good
personnel.

And so they know that somehow the problem must be
solved and the chasm closed as much as possible. But how?
Today, they are employing several methods that they hope
will contribute to the solution.

Take the matter of emotionally disturbed officers as an
example. Some hire or contract with psychiatrists and psy-
chologists to counsel the troubled officers. Some present
stress management programs; these programs feature
courses and individual guidance in techniques that can
help officers ease the frustrations, angers, and pressures felt
in their daily work. Further, all departments, in their academy and on-the-job training programs, are stressing the
need for a well-controlled behavior.[1]

To handle problems stemming from officer misconduct and the code of silence, the departments maintain Internal Affairs or Internal Investigation Divisions. And, to bring the police and the public to a better understanding of each other, a number of departments across the country have developed what are called police/community relations programs. In this chapter, we're going to look at the work of the Internal Affairs Divisions and at what is being attempted in the police/community relations programs.

INTERNAL AFFAIRS

Should you be charged with improper conduct or some breach of integrity, the matter will immediately go to Internal Affairs (IA) for a thorough investigation.[2] Should the investigation prove you to be guilty, your punishment will be decided elsewhere in the department—perhaps by the chief, perhaps by your immediate superiors, perhaps by a special disciplinary board of officials. IA limits itself only to the investigation and does not itself mete out whatever punishment is necessary. If requested by the department, however, it may help to decide on the needed punishment.

To meet its responsibilities, the Division takes on several jobs. It receives and records the charges against you; initiates and carries out the necessary investigation; presents its findings to the proper department authorities; and informs the people who brought the charges against you of what has been decided in the case.

Just who can bring charges against you? The answer: anyone with a complaint. Charges can be made by citizens, public officials, public and private agencies, and those of your fellow officers who cannot abide by the code of silence. In addition, the Division is able to investigate any misconduct or breach of integrity that it has come to suspect on its own. And it *must* investigate certain situations, among them the death or injury of a citizen at the hands of an officer, the death or injury of an officer at the hands of a citizen, and the firing of a weapon for any reason by an officer.

IA is charged with making its investigations in a fair and objective manner. It may not find a guilty officer innocent of an offense just because he or she is a fellow officer. Nor may it find an innocent officer guilty just to show the public how much the department hates misconduct. Two California cases indicate how closely the Division follows these rules.

In the city of Oakland, Internal Affairs recently investigated the shooting death of a sixteen-year-old boy. The death occurred when two officers attempted to stop a 1967 Cadillac for a traffic violation. The car sped off but was pulled to the curb after a two-minute chase. Two young men—the driver and a companion—jumped from the front seat and began to flee, with one of them drawing a loaded .38-caliber revolver and pointing it at the officers. One of the officers later claimed that he yelled, "Police! Halt! Freeze!" The shouts went ignored and the officer fired twice, hitting the boy with the revolver once in the left temple.

IA interviewed more than one hundred people during its investigation of the case. Of that number, six civilian witnesses stated that the youth was carrying a large handgun in his right hand as he exited the passenger side of the car. Eight said that they had heard the officer's warning shouts. No shots were fired at the other young man who had jumped from the front seat; he was subsequently arrested. Nor were shots fired at a passenger in the rear seat. He did not leave the car and was not arrested. On the basis of all this evidence, the officer was found innocent of wrongdoing.[3]

In nearby San Francisco, Internal Affairs was faced with the case of the rookies who, with some veteran officers, got into trouble while celebrating their graduation from the police academy. Liquor flowed freely and the party turned ugly when one young graduate was tied to a chair and made to submit to the advances of a prostitute hired by

Police officers
demonstrate too.

one of the veterans. The incident led to a number of officers, veterans and graduates alike, being accused of lewd and unprofessional conduct. Some were discharged from the department; others were suspended from duty for a period of time in the wake of the IA investigation.

Internal Affairs and
the Code of Silence

No matter how dedicated and objective they may be in their work, IA units cannot do a thorough job as long as the code of silence keeps officers from speaking up during investigations or reporting incidents that should be investigated. And so what can be done to end the code of silence?

Steps are being taken against it today, but it poses a knotty problem. The code is an old and deeply entrenched one in police work. Remember, virtually all officers hate the idea of being disloyal to fellow officers by snitching on them and, like the rest of us, have been taught that it is wrong to "tell on someone." Further, when they must speak out against a fellow officer, they are often up against the pain of pointing out someone who has become a close friend as well as a colleague over the years. Also, they may well find themselves hated, distrusted, and avoided by the men and women around them who do adhere to the code of silence. And so the efforts to be rid of it are certain to be long in bearing fruit.

Today, those efforts include the demands of many police commissioners and chiefs—among them Commissioner Benjamin Ward of New York City—that all citizen complaints no longer be buried in the station houses where they are received but be forwarded immediately to Internal Affairs.[4] Both the academy and on-the-job training in many departments are stressing that it is not mere snitching but a matter of basic professional integrity to speak out against officer behavior dangerous to the public and damaging to all law enforcement.

POLICE/COMMUNITY
RELATIONS PROGRAMS

As far back as twenty years ago, several departments began working on police/community relations programs. The years since have seen a growing number of departments join in this effort. The programs are aimed at reducing and preventing neighborhood crime and building a friendship and understanding between officers and the people they serve.

To reach these goals, the departments have tried various approaches. Officers have been sent to talk to school-children about the law and law enforcement work. During their off-duty hours, officers have coached amateur sports teams and served as officials at sports meets. They have volunteered as counselors in Boy and Girl Scout programs.

The departments have also devised various systems meant to provide specific protections for the public. Developed, for instance, was the now widely used system by which the people of the community can stamp their driving license numbers, their initials, or some other identifying mark on many of their belongings. In addition, the people can make lists of such "unstampable" possessions as certain pieces of jewelry and place them (along with photographs and written descriptions of the items) in a bank safe deposit box or some other secure location. The stamped items deter thieves from taking them, while the list of "unstampables," on being handed to the department after a burglary, makes it difficult for the culprit to "fence" (sell to an underworld buyer) the stolen goods.

To help in identifying babies and children, many departments have inaugurated programs for fingerprinting youngsters free of charge. If the child is later kidnapped or

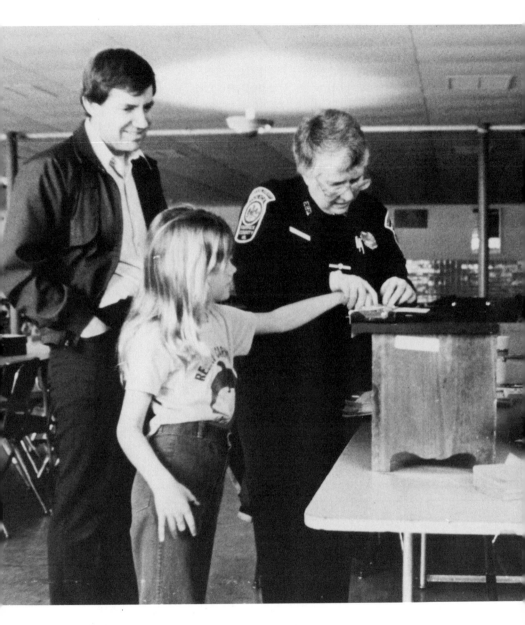

Fingerprinting children helps investigators track them in case they get lost or kidnapped.

lost, there is a fine tool for identification ready at hand. The service has proven especially helpful in identifying missing children who turn up years later.

In many communities, the departments have organized *block alert* programs. Behind these programs is the strategy of neighbors watching out for each other and for each other's possessions. A block alert program takes shape when the people on a street, in a neighborhood, or in an apartment house get together for a meeting with an officer. The officer talks to them about proper locks on doors, steps to follow if an intruder ever breaks in, and antiburglary measures to be taken before leaving home on a vacation. Each household is then given a block alert sticker and places it in a conspicuous spot on a window. The sticker lets would-be troublemakers know that neighbors have their eyes open for any unusual happenings and will summon the police at the first sign that something is amiss.

Help from the Press

The press is as aware of the police-public chasm as are the police themselves. Realizing that much news space and time has always been given to sensational crime stories, the news media have attempted to help close the chasm by devoting an increasing amount of attention to "good" stories that will "shine up" the police image—stories, for instance, along the lines of the recent one about the precinct officers who helped the thirteen-year-old victim of a bike theft. The boy needed the bike to earn money delivering newspapers so that he could send his younger, handicapped brother to a summer camp. The officers took up a collection and bought him a new bicycle.[5]

Another story that received much news attention concerned the man who wanted to adopt a dog from the local pound. He was to receive the dog free of charge, but found that he had to pay for a license and rabies shots. Living on a small income and unable to meet these expenses, the man broke into the pound one night and tried to steal the dog, only to be apprehended and arrested. He told the police that he wanted that particular animal because it reminded him of his former pet, a longtime companion that had been recently hit and killed by a car. The station officers responded with sympathy. They raised the money for the necessary expenses. Then they successfully urged the court not to sentence the man for burglary but to place him on two years' probation instead. In speaking of their efforts, one sergeant told reporters that his men were used to arresting people who didn't care about the property of others, but that they had no desire to send someone to prison for trying to get a dog.[6]

A Return to Earlier Ways

During the late 1970s and early 1980s, in answer to the criticism that the police were cold and aloof, intimidating in their leather-jacketed uniforms, and locked away in their cars, various cities tried to reestablish the image of the officer of the precar era—the friendly cop walking a beat. While not actually taking their officers out from behind the wheel, the departments urged their patrol personnel to stop whenever possible and leave their cruisers for the purpose of becoming more visible and approachable. In addition, the departments made a concerted effort to court the press and open the way to an increasing number of "good" police stories. These approaches showed promise for a time, but many were eventually abandoned, either because of lack of deep interest or changes in the personnel behind the movements.

Then the city of Newark, New Jersey, began experiments with the idea of actually putting foot officers on the streets.[7] These officers were instructed to be friendly and help the public in every way possible. In brief, each was to be part law enforcement officer and part social worker. Each was to help unite the police and the public and thus build a relationship of mutual trust that, in its turn, would see them working together to solve community troubles and combat neighborhood crime.

As *Newsweek* magazine reported in early 1985, the experiment did not produce any marked decline in Newark's crime rate, but it did succeed in reducing neighborhood hooliganism. It gave the residents an increased feeling of security. Created was an appreciation for the police that made the foot-patrol officers a welcome addition to the community. And, quite as important, it led to a highly successful police/community relations effort in nearby New York City.

Project CPOP

In mid-1984, the New York City Police Department launched a program called the Community Patrol Officer Program. The title meant that officers would put a strong emphasis on working to meet the community's general and specific needs. Known by the acronym CPOP, the program was first tried by one of the Department's Brooklyn precincts. Soon, seven more precincts were added to the program. At the time of this book's writing, fifty-five of the Department's seventy-five precincts are involved.

The project involved dividing a precinct into beats, each ranging in size from sixteen to thirty square blocks and assigning a Community Patrol officer to each. Working on foot, the officers were to get acquainted with the local residents, attend community meetings, organize block associations, and do whatever else was necessary to identify crime and "quality of life" problems in the neighborhoods. Then they were to set about helping to correct whatever problems had been turned up. The areas were much bothered with street hoodlums and a primary goal was to take the neighborhoods back from the hoodlums and return them to the residents.

To get the job done, the CPOP officers took on—and

124

have taken on ever since—a variety of assignments. They've worked with the city's sanitation department to clean out filthy empty lots and then have cooperated with the residents to turn them into playgrounds, small parks, or ball fields. They've dispersed bands of rowdies from street corners and have made it possible for people to pass by without being taunted or molested. They've gotten together with neighbors to host Halloween parties attended by more than 2,000 children, a strategem that has won the department a great deal of public goodwill and has put a stop to much of the night's vandalism. They've watched for and broken up street drug deals.

In all, CPOP has proven beneficial for both the public and the New York Department. The public trust of the officers has grown. The feeling of care for their neighborhoods has sharpened in the officers. Both sides have felt a pride in what they are doing. New York City police commissioner Benjamin Ward has remarked of the program, "When a police officer feels very protective about his people and the community feels they've got an officer they can trust, you've got something that works."

All, however, was not clear sailing for CPOP at first. When the project was launched, many residents were suspicious. They thought that the officers who appeared at the door to introduce the program were not officers at all but were con men with some plan to cheat them of money. It took the new arrivals some time to establish the public trust and liking widely seen today.

CPOP was designed by the Vera Institute of Justice, a nonprofit New York City organization that devotes itself to developing new techniques for improving the administration of criminal justice. It works with the police, courts, and public and private agencies to test innovative ways to safeguard defendants' rights, save money and man-hours for official agencies, and provide greater security and service for the public.[8]

The approach used in CPOP has proved so successful

*A police officer who is part of
the Community Patrol Officer
Program in Brooklyn, New York*

that other departments have adopted the program or projects of a similar nature. Among the departments that have done so are those in Boston, Chicago, Detroit, Houston, Minneapolis, Washington, D.C., and, in southern California, Orange County and the city of San Diego.

The city of Chicago has enjoyed success with its *Operation Crime-Stop.* The program involves citizens in combatting crime by urging them to call a special emergency telephone number to report suspicious occurrences; the information is then relayed to the authorities. Commendations are awarded to people whose calls prove of assistance to the police.

The police in Washington, D.C. have organized a citizen anticrime radio network. Taxi drivers and other people with radios in their cars are recruited to help the police by transmitting information regarding crimes and criminals.[9]

One of the earliest and most innovative of the CPOP and CPOP-like programs is to be found in San Diego.

CPOP IN SAN DIEGO

The San Diego Police Department's program, which first took shape in 1974, shares the aims of other CPOP projects.[10] It works to solve community problems and to serve the people with professional courtesy and thoughtful understanding. But it takes two additional steps. It calls for its officers to dress in a manner not intimidating to the public and urges them to devise programs of benefit to police/community relations.

The San Diego Uniform

San Diego's 1,300 sworn officers do not quite look like the personnel on most other American police forces. Their uniform is appropriate for the climate and lifestyle of a southern California city. Tan in color, it consists of sharply creased trousers and a short-sleeved, open-necked shirt worn over a white T-shirt (and armored vest). All accessories—shoes and gunbelt—are black. No department insignia, other than a gold badge and a small brass name plate, is to be seen. Nor are service bars sewn on the sleeves; for each five years of service, a small symbol, called a starship, appears on the name tag. The absence of decoration is due to Chief William Kolender's dislike of what he calls the "Boy Scout look" that patches and bars can give. He feels that they put a barrier between the officer and the public. For the same reason, the uniform has no stripes down the sides of the trousers.

Additionally, Kolender forbids the wearing of black gloves and mirror sunglasses because they give officers an intimidating look. Ordinary sunglasses are permitted.

The officers are not required to wear a hat. They keep helmets in the trunks of their patrol cars and use them only while directing traffic or dealing with an emergency. Chief Kolender wants his officers to appear human and to strike the public as individuals.

127

As for other equipment, officers have shotguns in their patrol cars and carry on their person a canister of Mace, a short wooden baton, and a revolver. An officer may carry a basic Smith and Wesson sidearm with a 6-inch barrel or may purchase and carry another model of his or her choice providing that it fires a conventional round-nosed .38-caliber Special bullet. Disliking gaping "dumdum" wounds, the department rejects the hollow-point ammunition favored by some police forces. The San Diego philosophy recognizes the need for guns but wants nothing to do with "overkill."

Even the department cruisers differ from the ones in most other cities. Instead of the usual "black-and-whites," which Chief Kolender believes are as intimidating as black gloves and mirror sunglasses, the cars are average-sized four-door white sedans and are fitted with such standard gear as a spotlight, radio aerial, and rooftop light bar. The front doors are painted with the city's crest and the words *To Protect and Serve.*

Police/Community Relations

Ever since its inception, the San Diego program has urged officers to think up police/community relations ideas to better the department's public image and improve its effectiveness in working with the people.

Among the ideas that have been put into practice is the *ride-along* program, which enables members of the public to join officers on patrol. The program is available to anyone who is interested as long as the person lives or works within the area being patrolled. When first suggested, it was a completely new concept in community relations and

*Foot officers on the
beat in San Diego*

met with resistance from the administrative officials in the city government. One of their chief objections was the possibility that the passengers would distract the officers from their duties.

Nevertheless, the idea was given a try and has proven successful. At present, it is quite commonplace to see a patrol officer and civilian pulling a shift together. The rider might be a teacher, a social worker, an ordinary citizen, a juvenile who is causing trouble, or a teenager curious about police work or interested in joining a force one day. The officer tries to show the rider what police work is all about and what policemen and policewomen are really like. In turn, the rider can educate the officer about the neighborhood and some of the problems it faces. The department feels that there is a lasting benefit for both.

THE PROGRAMS:
PRAISE AND CRITICISM

The various programs—from the block alert programs to the CPOP and CPOP-like projects—are widely considered to have been successes. But this is not to say that everyone is pleased with them. They have been the targets of criticism as well as praise. Let's look now at what has been said on both sides of the fence.[11]

*The Block Alert and
Identification Programs*

Now to be found in cities all across the nation, the block alert programs are said to have proven themselves successful on three counts. They've discouraged burglaries, particularly those committed by small-time amateurs. They've given a protection above and beyond that which police patrols can be expected o provide. And, of utmost importance in cities where even next-door neighbors can be complete strangers, they have created bonds of friendship among the residents and have generated the healthy feeling that comes with caring for one another.

On the other side of the fence, there is the feeling that the block alert and identification (of personal valuables and such) programs are of only limited value. While they are doing some good, they are failing to stem the tide of crime in the United States. Many critics of the programs believe that the money and officer time expended on them would be better spent on police duties more directly related to the apprehension of criminals. For example, the critics feel that a department's money and time would better go to increasing police patrols and providing more manpower for investigations.

There is also the feeling that crime prevention is actually of secondary importance in the programs. Critics here say that the departments know the programs to be of limited value and use them mainly as public relations ploys to make themselves look good. The police deny this charge. While saying that no one program can hope to be a cure-all for the nation's crime problem, they argue that the programs are being of some help and that this help is certainly better than no help at all. And they point out the successes that many of the programs have recorded in reducing hooliganism and other problems in their neighborhoods and bringing the police and public closer together.

While the value of the programs may be a matter of debate, there is no question that one of their number has failed and has proven a headache to the police. Some years ago, when the car and the radio promised to deter and reduce crime by providing speedy responses to trouble, the police established an emergency telephone number nationwide—911. Because it could be easily memorized, they believed that a person would quickly dial the number when in trouble and thus hasten even more their responses.

*Police officers and participants in
a Neighborhood Watch program*

But things did not work out as planned. Very soon, the number was being deluged with every type of call imaginable. Many had little or nothing to do with genuine emergencies. People, for example, called to report broken parking meters, to complain about weeds in vacant lots or nearby homes in need of painting, and even to ask why their Social Security checks had not arrived on time. Often, when there was an actual emergency, the caller could not get through because the line was busy. Though troublesome and jammed with nonessential calls, the emergency number remains in use today and is known by the nickname "Dial-A-Cop." The New York City Police Department yearly takes some 3 million 911 calls.[12]

CPOP Projects

A recent report from the Washington, D.C.-based Crime Control Institute points up one facet of the successes won by the CPOP and CPOP-like projects. Because they have enabled the police and public to get to know each other, the report holds that they have helped to reduce the violence long seen on both sides of the fence. It points out that in 1986 big-city officers killed half as many people in the line of duty as they did fourteen years earlier. Conversely, there was a reduction of two-thirds in the number of officers killed in the line of duty.

There is also no doubt that the projects have cut the number of other types of offenses. For instance, New York's CPOP project, remember, has made the sidewalks safer for pedestrians by dispersing street-corner rowdies and has reduced the amount of Halloween-night trouble with its block parties.

In the main, the officers involved in the projects are pleased with them. Some say that, now that the neighborhoods have gotten to know them, they are no longer struck with those hard epithets that have been heard since the turbulent 1960s—"pig" and "fascist." Others comment

133

that the programs give them the chance to follow up on people and their problems, rather than simply answer emergency calls as they come in and then, once they are cared for, move on to other matters. Most admit to a growing respect for themselves and their uniforms because of the work they see themselves doing in the neighborhoods.

But the projects have their detractors as well as their supporters. A general complaint here is the same as that leveled against the block alert and identification programs. It holds that the projects actually do little to stem the tide of crime in the country and have the smack of a public relations ploy to them.

Also, there are a number of specific doubts about the projects. Some critics fear the projects because, with officers mingling with the residents, there seems to be a great chance for corruption to develop. First, an officer becomes too friendly with the people on the beat. Then he or she takes advantage of them and their weaknesses by accepting bribes and payoffs or by simply looking the other way when an infraction of the law occurs.

Another criticism: by becoming friendly with the people, officers run the risk of thinking them all to be "nice" when in reality some are out-and-out crooks. A blindness occurs that makes it possible for even more crimes than ever before to be committed and go unpunished.

Regardless of the criticisms, however, the CPOP approach—the attempt to meet the community's needs and seek a firm union between the police and the public— seems to be here to stay. In the minds of many law enforcement officials, the idea of bringing officers and the community closer together is vital to the work of keeping our streets and neighborhoods safe and peaceful. But the job cannot be done by the police alone. It is a task in which they and the public must unite in a joint effort. Thus, as Lawrence Sherman of the Police Foundation, a nationwide law enforcement organization, sees it, the approach used in the CPOP programs and all like them is "the wave of the future in policing."

The Police
Two Rising Groups

In Chapter One, we spoke of two groups that long found it difficult, if not impossible, to enter police work—women and minority-group members. Due to a number of factors, they have been playing an increasing role in law enforcement in recent years. We turn now to them for a look at the problems they have faced—and, in many instances, still face—in winning that increasing role.

In the next pages, we'll report on each group in turn. We must first, however, talk about the factors that have brought them more and more into law enforcement after decades of being shunned.

THE BACKGROUND

Among its various provisions, the Fourteenth Amendment to the Constitution holds that no state may deny any person "the equal protection of the laws." This provision has been interpreted to mean that no one, for any reason, may be unfairly deprived of making a living. Despite the Amendment, which went into effect in 1865, women and minority-group members were denied easy access to many occupations, including law enforcement, during the subsequent decades. And those who did manage to enter the profession were restricted to certain jobs and found promotions hard, if not impossible at times, to come by.

Women were denied access, in the main, because their size and physical strength did not measure up to those thought necessary for policing. For many years, the average patrolman, unlike his counterpart of today, worked alone and not with a partner. He was expected to take care of all problems on his beat—from handling obstreperous drunks to breaking up street gangs—by himself. In fact, there was a stigma attached to requesting help from another officer. Consequently, the departments were always seeking big, burly men to serve as patrol officers. The official view was that the job was simply too physically demanding and dangerous for women, with their slighter builds—and too sordid for their delicate feminine natures. Police work had to be left to the man.

The minorities suffered from the racial bias that the departments (and other white-dominated occupations) shared with great segments of the white public. Much of the prejudice was directed at blacks. Dating back to the long decades of slavery and worsened by the wounds and memories of the Civil War, it was a prejudice that wrote blacks off as inferior and, by nature, inept. Additionally, such factors as cultural differences and limited educational opportunities caused not only the blacks but such other ethnic groups as the Hispanics and Asians to be regarded as "unreliable" and "backward" and thus unfit to wear a uniform.

The Civil Rights Act

The situation began to change some thirty years ago for both women and the minority members. The change was prompted by the civil rights movement of the 1950s.

Headed principally by the nation's black population, it led to the passage of the 1964 Civil Rights Act by the United States Congress.[1] One section of the Act—called Title VII—struck at the prejudicial measures traditionally practiced by many employers. It prohibited discrimination because of race, sex, color, religion, or national origin in employment matters. The prohibition embraced all areas of employment, from hiring and salary to promotion and dismissal.

Title VII was strengthened considerably in several ways when it was amended in 1972 and became the Equal Employment Opportunity Act. For one, the U.S. Department of Justice was empowered to sue state and local governments for violations of fair employment practices. Today, under the terms of the Act, the federal government, the states, and individuals can sue employers for failing to observe fair employment procedures.

In 1965, just months after the passage of the Civil Rights Act, President Lyndon B. Johnson issued an executive order calling for all federal contractors and subcontractors to develop what he called *affirmative action* programs in their employment practices. Though at first directed only at firms doing business with the federal government, the idea of affirmative action has been taken up by the states over the years. Today, the term means any policy or program designed to increase the number of minority-group members or of women in careers or schools from which they have previously been wholly or greatly excluded.

It is under the Civil Rights Act and the affirmative action programs that women and minorities have been able to play an increasing part in police work. But both groups have faced difficulties.

WOMEN IN POLICE WORK

Women have been involved in American police work for just over a century now.[2] Their participation began in 1884

137

when the New York City Police Department hired its first female officer and assigned her to a duty that male officers and certain of their prisoners had always found difficult and embarrassing. She was made a police "matron," her job being to search, guard, and supervise women prisoners.

In the next years, other departments joined New York City in realizing that women had at least a limited value in police work. Women were hired as clerks and as officers meant to deal with adult female offenders, teenage girls, and young children (ten years or younger) of both sexes. For example, in 1893, the mayor of Chicago appointed Mrs. Marie Owens, a patrolman's widow, to the job of assisting with courtroom cases involving women and children. Then, in 1910, the Los Angeles department employed Mrs. Alice Stebbins Wells and gave her the job of policing recreation spots popular with the young—skating rinks, penny arcades, dance halls, and movie theaters. She also assisted with missing person cases.

The tradition of the proud male officer who was able to handle all emergencies by himself kept the women tied to their limited duties for many years. But, with the emergence of the police cruiser and the radio, it slowly faded and become a thing of the past. The departments, much for safety's sake, began to assign two-man teams to the cruisers, a practice that is still followed in many communities today. As for the radio, it enabled backup units to come to an officer's assistance in a matter of minutes. There was no longer the need for that I-can-take-care-of-it-by-myself patrolman. A door to a wider variety of duties for the woman was opening.

Then, in the mid-1960s, came the Civil Rights Act and President Johnson's call for affirmative action programs. Ever since the nineteenth century, great numbers of women had been demanding certain rights—among them the right to vote and the right to equal employment opportunities with the male. They had won the vote in 1920 with the ratification of the Nineteenth Amendment to the Constitution. Title VII of the Civil Rights Act and then the affirm-

138

ative action programs enabled them to press even harder for the long-sought right to equal employment opportunities.

Policewomen Today

Over the past twenty years, police departments in all states have assigned women to unrestricted duties.[3] They work today as patrol officers, detectives, mechanics, and laboratory scientists, and have won promotions to the ranks of sergeant, lieutenant, and captain. For several years in the 1980s, Portland, Oregon, had a woman chief of police. In New Orleans, a woman serves with a SWAT (Special Weapons and Tactics) team. Between 1975 and 1978, the provost marshal (a military chief of police) at Fort Knox, Kentucky, was a woman. She headed a force of four hundred and held the rank of colonel.

All this is not meant to say that women have become, in terms of numbers, a major force in police work. They remain solidly in the minority among law enforcement employees. In 1985, they accounted for only 20.6 percent of the total police personnel (sworn officers and civilian workers) at the local, county, and state levels, while 79.4 percent of the jobs were held by men. Among sworn officers, their number was even smaller—6.8 percent as opposed to 93.2 percent for men. Only in one area were they in the majority; they represented 64.1 percent of the civilian employees in law enforcement, with men trailing well behind at 35.9 percent.[4]

Though still in the minority, women are being increasingly recruited today—a fact that can be seen by comparing two of the above statistics with a corresponding figure from four years earlier. While women accounted for only 20.6 percent of all police employees in 1985, they were worse off in 1981, when their percentage stood at 17.9. The 1981 percentage for women sworn officers was 5.5 as compared with 6.8 in 1985.

The increased recruitment of women has not, however, seen them happily welcomed by all departments and all male officers. Many women, yes, admit to being treated as equals by their male colleagues, but others speak of being shunned, resented, and too often overlooked for promotion. The resentment is especially prevalent among those "macho" men who still cling to the old tradition of the tough, brawny, able-to-handle-anything officer; who believe that the police world is an exclusively male world; and who regard women as intruders on that domain.

Instances of this attitude at work have been seen time and again.[5] A policewoman recently told of riding in a van transporting several prisoners to jail. When the vehicle braked to a stop at its destination, she jumped out to pull open the heavy rear sliding door. A male officer standing nearby came to lend a hand, only to have the driver lean out the window and say, "Leave her be. She's making as much money as us. Let her open her own door."

Another policewoman remembers the night she was struggling with a drunken, belligerent teenager. "I had the girl almost to the patrol car when suddenly she broke loose and whirled around. She grabbed my arm and sank her teeth into it. I tell you, it hurt like the dickens. I finally got her subdued and into the unit. But I was sure mad. Two policemen had been standing across the street watching us. Neither one of them made a move to help. When I asked them why, one of them said, "Hey, dolly, if you can't do a man's work, go back to your knitting."

Still another policewoman tells of how, before booking a prisoner at her station house, she placed her sidearm in

Top: *The 1969 police academy graduation class in Fairfax County, Virginia.* Bottom: *The 1987 graduation class in Fairfax County.*

an unlocked storage compartment (a procedure used by many departments to safeguard against prisoners who might take it into their heads to grab for the weapon). When she returned to the compartment, she found that someone had emptied the gun of its bullets—a stunt that could have proved fatal had she later encountered a situation requiring the use of arms. The culprit has never been exposed, but is strongly suspected to have been a man. Later, she received an anonymous note warning her not to take the next examination for promotion to sergeant. Again, though the culprit has remained unknown, the writer is thought to have been a male.

In addition to such incidents as these, there have been occasions when a woman officer's call for backup assistance has not been answered as quickly as possible. Some policewomen have run up against sexist graffiti on station walls and have complained of being deliberately subjected to crude jokes. Others have told of male officers excluding them from discussions of crime problems in the area and of planned drug raids. Many have made claims of being sexually harassed by their male colleagues (it must also be reported that some say they have never been troubled with sexual harassment).[6]

Not all the antagonism comes from the macho-type policeman. Many male officers feel that they have legitimate concerns over the growing presence of policewomen. For one, there is the criticism that, to open the way for women, many a department has lowered its employment standards—especially those pertaining to physical prowess—and thus has reduced its ability to do the best job possible for the community. Another concern is that the presence of a woman in a dangerous situation may cause the male to become protective of her and thus unduly endanger his own safety.[7]

That these concerns may, at least in part, be groundless is indicated in recent studies of policewomen. The studies, which began in the early 1970s, have sought to compare the performance of male and female officers who do the same job and share the same amount of experience. They have shown that in most areas the men and women are equally effective. In certain other areas (for one, sheer physical strength), the men are somewhat more effective, and in still others, the women win out.[8]

The women have proven themselves especially effective in cases dealing with children, and with female suspects or witnesses. The studies also show that the citizens with whom the women have dealt think them to be more sensitive and sympathetic than the men and are thus able to settle a difficult matter all the more quickly and gracefully.[9]

THE MINORITIES IN POLICE WORK

Though a variety of minority groups are represented in law enforcement, black officers earn the most mention in the press and in police studies. Like women, they have been involved in policing since the late 1800s. The first mention of a black officer is found in the personnel records of the Washington, D.C. department for 1861.[10]

Because of the various prejudices earlier mentioned, the minorities were not heavily recruited for the police until the years following the civil rights movement. Since then, there has been an effort to bring them into the departments. But the picture of their recruitment is one of sharp contrasts. In some ways, they seem to have been employed in great number. In other ways, the number recruited seems insignificant.

Recruitment: The Contrasts

Pamela D. Mayhall, in *Police-Community Relations and the Administration of Justice*, reports that blacks have been increasingly employed by departments since the 1940s.

143

She writes that between 1960 and 1970 the employment of black officers increased approximately 138 percent over the preceding decade, while the estimated number of all police officers recruited increased only 33 percent.[11] In contrast, *Statistical Abstract of the United States, 1986* reports that nationwide the number of black and other minority officers remains low—under 9 percent (5.3 percent for blacks, 2.9 percent for Hispanics, and a miniscule percentage for Asians).[12] But then we come upon another contrast.

The above figures, remember, represent the nation as a whole. The percentages vary widely when we turn to individual cities. Some cities carry a heavy percentage of minority officers, while the percentage is slight in others. Florida's Miami Police Department stands at one extreme here; 58.6 percent of the force is represented by the minorities (the figure is divided between 17.1 percent for blacks and, because of the city's extremely large Latin population, 41.5 percent for Hispanics). The same holds true for Oakland, California (over 22 percent), and Washington, D.C. (over 45 percent). At the opposite end of the scale, the minorities, as shown by the following figures from the early 1980s, have been poorly represented in Boston (3.9 percent) and Houston (4.3 percent).[13]

Minority Officers–Minority Groups

Regardless of the wide variance in the statistics, the fact remains that minority officers in no locale equal the percentage of minority groups living there. The minority officers and many white police officials see this as regrettable on two counts. First, they feel that the ethnic groups are not being given the equal employment opportunities that the law requires, a situation that seems especially sad in organizations dedicated to upholding the law in all ways.

Their second belief stems from the fact that most—if

not all—minority groups feel that white officers discriminate against them in attitude and treatment. It is believed that minority officers would handle the minority populations with greater fairness and sympathy, and that the minority populations would show a greater cooperation when dealing with officers of "their own kind."

There is, however, a doubt as to whether minority officers are actually fairer and more sympathetic than white officers.[14] Several recent studies of black officers have indicated that they can be both harsh and prejudicial when dealing with black suspects. One study reported that both black and white policemen are more likely to employ undue force against members of their own race.

And what of the belief that the minority populations would react in a cooperative fashion with minority officers? The above studies have cast a doubt on its validity. They indicate that black officers are the subjects of mixed emotions here. Some black citizens interviewed for the studies felt that black officers would have a deeper understanding of the community's problems and would be responsible for better treatment of suspects and improved police/community relations. Other black citizens revealed they disliked, scorned, and mistrusted "their own kind" in uniform as much as they did whites.

Minority Officers Today

Many minority officers today feel that they occupy a strange position as law enforcement employees. As members of the minority populations, they feel separated from the white officers around them. As members of a police department, they feel separated from those great segments in the minority population that dislike and distrust them. In all, they feel a deep isolation within a profession that, as was explained in earlier chapters, itself feels isolated from the general population.

Their complaints of the treatment accorded them by their departments parallel those voiced by so many policewomen. They contend that they are too often overlooked for promotion. They point to a failure of cooperation on the parts of many of their white colleagues. They report being made to endure crude ethnic jokes. They claim to be left out of work discussions by white officers.

A recent study of the San Jose, California, Police Department can serve as an illustration of how the minority officers in many cities feel.[15] Twenty-eight of the department's thirty-one black officers were interviewed in the course of the study, which was conducted by a group known as Officers for a Better San Jose. When the results were made public in January, 1987, they brought to light the following complaints:

- During the past eleven years, San Jose has hired 302 officers, bringing its department strength to 1,008 men and women. In that period, the number of black officers has risen only from sixteen to thirty-one.

- Of the 249 supervisory positions in the department, a mere three are filled by blacks. Two of those positions are filled by sergeants, and one by a lieutenant.

- Of the black officers questioned for the report, fourteen said that they had felt the sting of discrimination at one time or another; the discriminations ranged from racial jokes at recent training academy graduation exercises to the failure to win promotions. Twelve black officers said they had never been the victims of discrimination. Two officers refused to answer questions on the topic.

The report has led to department discussions on possible remedies for the problems voiced by the black officers.

(NOTE: The department reports that its percentage of black officers is low—3.2—because San Jose does not have a large black population. The city's Hispanic population is much greater, with the result that Hispanic officers make up 22 percent of the department's personnel. The department also reports that it gives civil service examinations for advancement to supervisory positions and that a number of black officers have not been employed long enough to qualify for the exams.)

On the opposite side of the fence, many white officers across the nation argue that much of the antagonism directed against minority officers is not based on prejudice. Here, they make a charge that is also directed against policewomen: that many departments have lowered their employment standards—especially, in this instance, their educational requirements—to make room for minority officers with less education. This is seen as a major threat to police efficiency and professionalism.

Great segments of the police community are also disturbed by the *quota system* that many departments have adopted to make way for the minorities. The quota system calls for a certain percentage of minority members always to be among the officers recruited. It also demands that a certain percentage of the available promotions go to the minorities. These quotas must be met regardless of whether the minority applicants prove themselves as qualified as their white competitors. (The quotas also apply to women applicants for employment or promotion.)

The Los Angeles Police Department provides an example of the quota system at work. In 1980, at the end of an employment discrimination lawsuit brought by the U.S. Department of Justice, the department agreed that 45 percent of all new recruits would be black or Hispanic and that 20 percent would be women.[16]

The quota system is seen as vastly unfair by many whites. They argue that it all too often causes qualified whites to miss out on jobs and promotions that then go to less qualified minority representatives. It is also regarded by white personnel as damaging to the quality of police work and is widely known among them and many civilians as a *reverse discrimination*.

The legality of the quota system, which is also used in other public agencies and schools, has been under challenge for a number of years. Three quota cases have earned U.S. Supreme Court rulings, but these rulings have failed to give a clear answer to the question of whether the system is legal or illegal.

In the late 1970s, a young man named Allen Bakke brought a lawsuit against a California medical school for refusing to accept him as a student. He charged reverse discrimination because, under the institution's quota system, sufficient whites had already been enrolled and the next appointments had to be given to minority students. When his case went to the Supreme Court, it was decided that the school should accept him as a student. But the ruling proved to be a confusing one because it embraced two contrasting views. On the one hand, it held that quota systems cannot alone be used to govern enrollment or employment. But, on the other hand, it maintained that racial background must be a prime consideration in both matters. Employers were left without any real understanding as how to apportion jobs among the minorities and the whites.[17]

The situation was further muddled by the two other Supreme Court decisions. On the facts of a case before it in the early 1980s, the Court held that the quota system could be used. Then, in a 1987 quota case, the Court ruled that black officers must receive half the promotions awarded by the Alabama state police.

And so the quota's legality remains in question today, with many whites calling the system unfair, and many minority groups seeing it as the one strong means of insuring that their representatives are able to surmount the greater unfairness of employment discrimination. Police officials believe that the answer to the whole complex question can be reached only through a series of future court cases.

*   *   *

The employment, treatment, and promotions of police-women and minority officers is today a thorny problem in many departments. However, it is a problem that, despite its various troublesome aspects, seems to be slowly solving itself as the years pass and bring an increasing number of women and minority-group members into law enforcement. The hope is that it will soon be totally a thing of the past, for those presently in law enforcement work are making—and those who follow them will certainly make—significant contributions to the role of the police in our society.

Epilogue
The Police of the Future

This book has dealt with the role played today in our society by the municipal police officer and department. In these closing pages, we must turn to another topic. What does the future hold for law enforcement in the United States?

Police officials who are concerned with the future predict that the coming years will bring great changes in both the methods of policing and the very nature of the work itself. Many of the changes are expected to be here by the dawn of the twenty-first century, which lies just a handful of years over the horizon.

POLICE METHODS

The methods of policing will be much altered by advances in the technical gear already being used by many departments.[1] Two prime examples of such gear are television and the computer. Some predictions hold that the TV camera may well reduce the need for officers to patrol a beat.

In increasing number, closed-circuit cameras will be installed in places of business and connected to police headquarters. Station personnel will monitor them throughout the day and night. Patrol cars and helicopters will be dispatched at the first sign of trouble at any location.

There are even predictions that television will eliminate the need for officers to gather at their stations for roll-call training before going on duty. By means of what is called *teleconferencing*, groups of officers will receive the instruction and information that make up roll-call training via closed-circuit monitors in their own homes and then go on duty from there. This type of arrangement is seen as especially valuable for suburban departments that are able to employ just a few men but must often patrol sprawling neighborhood areas. Saved will be a trip to the station house and then a journey back out to an officer's distant beat.

As for the computer, its uses—as they already are—will be many. They will range from collecting and storing information to providing a lightninglike communication between departments and their officers and between the officers themselves. Patrol cars will be equipped with computers so that, while remaining behind the wheel, an officer can instantly call up needed data on a suspicious person or vehicle.

A number of law enforcement officials worry, however, that increasing computerization may lead to a new type of police corruption. The fear is that the vast amount of criminal information stored in computer files may be misused by anyone with access to it. For example, a single misdeed or thoughtless misstep in the past may leave an otherwise law-abiding citizen open to blackmail at the hands of an unscrupulous officer.

Other items of gear that are expected to play an increasing role in the future include: helicopters and fast-moving, highly maneuverable three-wheel cars for traffic control; robots for storming criminal hideaways or build-

A remote-controlled police bomb squad
robot reaches for a dynamite bomb.

ings where hostages are being held prisoner (robots are presently being used for traffic control in some cities); and "space backpacks" that will allow an officer, in the style of comic-strip hero Buck Rogers, to hover above the scene of an accident, crime, or public disturbance.

THE NATURE OF POLICE WORK

And what of the very nature of police work?[2] James R. Metts, the sheriff of South Carolina's Lexington County, has written on this topic in a 1985 issue of *The Futurist* magazine. In an article entitled "The Police Force of Tomorrow," he predicts that:

> *Officers will serve a society much different than the one we know today. They will be faced with an increasing minority population, with increasing numbers of children being raised in single-parent households, and with more and more people living in small towns and suburban areas. Hence, it will be their duty to provide services specifically needed by and of value to each of these diverse groups.*
>
> *With the human life span increasing as it is, there will be more elderly people in the nation than ever before. The police will be called on to serve their needs. Officers, for example, will need to be experts in the paramedic services often required by the aged.*
>
> *Departments will put a decided emphasis on recruiting well-educated officers, officers who are capable of handling successfully a wide variety of peace-keeping, community, and social service duties, not to mention the increasingly complicated technical gear with which their departments will*

154

be armed. The emphasis on well-educated officers will also be aimed at dignifying police work and improving its public image. Thus, future advancement in a department will depend more heavily on qualifications and education rather than years of service, as is so often the case today.

As is happening at present, police leaders will continue to strive toward having law enforcement recognized not simply as a line of work but as a "true" profession, such as medicine and engineering. They look to the day when a college diploma will be required for employment and when university students will welcome the police recruiter to their campuses as eagerly as they now welcome recruiters from other fields.

More and more women and minority officers will be recruited as the prejudices of the past and present are replaced by a deeper understanding and appreciation of the services these officers can perform.

Tomorrow's police will require new technical skills and insights to handle criminal problems that are just beginning to be seen today—problems such as computer thefts, electronic banking card thefts, international political terrorism, and the misuse of scientific developments.

In all, as they are today and have been for years, the police in the future will be, to use Sheriff Metts's word, the "caretakers" of our society. But it will be an even more complex society than the one we know today. And so their role in it will demand that they be more highly trained than ever before in human psychology; community and ethnic needs; social, legal, and technical matters; and their own

personal sense of worth, responsibility, and professionalism.

It is a role that can be described in only one way:
necessary for our society's well-being and challenging for
the police.

Notes

CHAPTER ONE

1. Material on the duties of the police officer to maintain public order and enforce the law is developed from Thomas F. Adams, *Police Field Operations* (Englewood Cliffs, N.J.: Prentice-Hall, 1985), pp. 2, 5, 7, 9–10; Thomas F. Adams, *Law Enforcement: An Introduction to the Police Role in the Community* (Englewood Cliffs: N.J., Prentice-Hall, 1968), pp. 84–85; Ronald J. Waldron, *The Criminal Justice System: An Introduction*, 3d ed. (Boston: Houghton Mifflin, 1984), pp. 171–173; Charles E. Silberman, *Criminal Violence, Criminal Justice* (New York: Random House, 1978), pp. 202–204. Additional information on the subject may be obtained from these sources and from Clemens Bartollas, Stuart J. Miller, and Paul C. Wice, *Participants in the Criminal Justice System: The Promise and the Performance* (Englewood Cliffs, N.J.: Prentice-Hall, 1983), pp. 91–95.
2. Material on the police officer's referral duties is developed from conversations with Maurice Lafferty, Associate Professor, Administration of Justice Program, Marin Community College, Kentfield, Calif.
3. Silberman, *Criminal Violence, Criminal Justice*, p. 204.
4. George D. Eastman, ed., *Municipal Police Administration* (Washington: International City Management Association, 1969), p. 321.

5. *Uniform Crime Reports for the United States* (Washington: Federal Bureau of Investigation, U.S. Department of Justice, 1986), p. 41.
6. "Detroit Man Gets $1 Million in Police Brutality Case," *Jet*, May 4, 1987, p. 29.
7. "Miami Vice: Sorting Good Guys from Bad Guys," *U.S. News & World Report*, February 2, 1987, p. 28.

CHAPTER TWO

1. *The New Book of Knowledge*, vol. 15 (Danbury, Conn.: Grolier, 1983), p. 372.
2. Floyd James Torbet, *Policemen the World Over* (New York: Hastings House, 1965), pp. 12–16.
3. Material on the police in early Great Britain is developed from Walter Arm, *The Policeman: An Inside Look at His Role in a Modern Society* (New York: Dutton, 1969), pp. 14–15; Thomas F. Adams, *Law Enforcement: An Introduction to the Police Role in the Community* (Englewood Cliffs, N.J.: Prentice-Hall, 1968), pp. 19–36. Additional information on the subject may be obtained from Ronald J. Waldron, *The Criminal Justice System: An Introduction*, 3d ed. (Boston: Houghton Mifflin, 1984), chapter five, pp. 118–130. The chapter provides a concise and thorough history of British and American policing.
4. Material on Robert Peel is developed from Adams, *Law Enforcement*, pp. 60–62; Pamela D. Mayhall, *Police-Community Relations and the Administration of Justice* (New York: John Wiley, 1967), p. 14; A. C. Germann, Frank D. Day, and Robert R. J. Gallati, *Introduction to Law Enforcement and Criminal Justice*, rev. 6th printing (Springfield, Ill.: Charles C. Thomas, 1968), pp. 59–62.
5. Material on the early American watch and ward system and the first paid police is developed from Arm, *The Policeman*, pp. 14–15; Samuel Walker, *The Police in America: An Introduction* (New York: McGraw-Hill, 1983), pp. 6–7; Germann, Day, and Gallati, *Introduction to Law Enforcement and Criminal Justice*, pp. 64–67.
6. Material on U.S. police corruption in the 1800s and the passage of the Pendleton Civil Service Act is developed from Walker, *The Police in America*, pp. 7, 84; Germann, Day, and Gallati, *Introduction to Law Enforcement and Criminal Justice*, pp. 65–66.
7. Robert M. Fogelson, *Big-City Police* (Cambridge, Mass.: Harvard University Press, 1977), p. 129.
8. Fogelson, p. 148.
9. Ralph Lee Smith, *The Tarnished Badge* (New York: Thomas Y. Crowell, 1965), p. 168.

10. Smith, p. 169.
11. *Uniform Crime Reports for the United States* (Washington: Federal Bureau of Investigation, U.S. Department of Justice, 1986), p. 242.
12. Arm, *The Policeman*, p. 22.

CHAPTER THREE

1. *Uniform Crime Reports for the United States* (Washington: Federal Bureau of Investigation, U.S. Department of Justice, 1986), pp. 242, 248.
2. Material on police employment standards and training is developed from Thomas F. Adams, *Law Enforcement: An Introduction to the Police Role in the Community* (Englewood Cliffs, N.J.: Prentice-Hall, 1968), pp. 19–36; Walter Arm, *The Policeman: An Inside Look at His Role in a Modern Society* (New York: Dutton, 1968), pp. 56–65; conversations with Maurice Lafferty, Associate Professor, Administration of Justice Program, Marin Community College, Kentfield, Calif.
3. Arm, *The Policeman*, pp. 24–25; A. C. Germann, Frank D. Day, and Robert R. J. Gallati, *Introduction to Law Enforcement and Criminal Justice*, rev. 6th printing (Springfield, Ill.: Charles C. Thomas, 1968), p. 66.
4. Todd S. Purdom, "Every Police Bullet Fired Must Pass Many Layers of Inquiry," *The New York Times*, January 25, 1987.
5. Personal knowledge of the authors.
6. David Maraniss, "When the Law Turns Outlaw," *San Francisco Chronicle/Examiner*, October 5, 1986.
7. Material on public-police debate concerning police use of the gun is developed from conversations with Maurice Lafferty.
8. Maraniss, "When the Law Turns Outlaw."
9. Provided by Kevin Mullen, Deputy Chief of Police (retired), San Francisco Police Department.
10. Adams, *Law Enforcement*, pp. 216–217.

CHAPTER FOUR

1. Material on the United States Constitution and the Bill of Rights is developed from *Constitution of the United States, Constitution of California and Related Documents* (Sacramento, Calif.: California State Senate, 1977), pp. 35–62; Thomas F. Adams, *Law Enforcement: An Introduction to the Police Role in the Community* (Englewood Cliffs, N.J.: Prentice-Hall, 1968), pp. 201–211; George D. Eastman, ed., *Municipal Police Administration*, 6th ed. (Wash-

ington: International City Management Association, 1969), pp. 10–12; A. C. Germann, Frank D. Day, and Robert R. J. Gallati, *Introduction to Law Enforcement and Criminal Justice*, rev. 6th printing (Springfield, Ill.: Charles C. Thomas, 1968), pp. 102–106, 239–240; and Maurice Lafferty, Associate Professor, Criminal Justice Program, Marin Community College, Kentfield, Calif. Additional information on the U.S. Constitution and the Bill of Rights can be obtained from Ronald J. Waldron, *The Criminal Justice System: An Introduction*, 3d ed. (Boston: Houghton Mifflin, 1984), appendix B, pp. 517–534.

2. Material on the Skokie Park case is developed from Aryeh Neier, *Defending My Enemy* (New York: Dutton, 1979), prologue, chapters 1, 3, 4, 7, and epilogue.

3. *The People's Almanac* (New York: Doubleday, 1975), p. 254; *The People's Almanac II* (New York: Morrow, 1978), p. 474.

4. Material on the *Escobedo* decision is developed from: Germann, Day, and Gallati, *Introduction to Law Enforcement and Criminal Justice*, p. 102; *World Book Encyclopedia*, vol. 6 (Chicago: World Book, 1984), p. 275.

5. Material on the *Miranda* decision and guidelines is developed from Adams, *Law Enforcement*, pp. 209–210; *Academic American Encyclopedia*, vol. 13 (Princeton, N.J.: Arete, 1981), p. 463; *The New Encyclopaedia Britannica*, vol. 8 [Ready Reference] (Chicago: Encyclopaedia Britannica, 1986), p. 180; *Encyclopedia Americana*, vol. 19 (Danbury, Conn.: Grolier, 1984), p. 220; Clemens Bartollas, Stuart J. Miller, and Paul B. Wice, *Participants in American Criminal Justice: The Promise and the Performance* (Englewood Cliffs, N.J.: Prentice-Hall, 1983), pp. 178–179; Fred E. Inbau, "Over-Reaction—The Mischief of Miranda v. Arizona," *FBI Law Enforcement Bulletin*, April 1983, pp. 22–29. Additional information on the subject may be obtained from Thomas F. Adams, *Police Field Operations* (Englewood Cliffs, N.J.: Prentice-Hall, 1985), chapter 6, pp. 180–185. These pages provide a discussion of the interrogation techniques to be followed under the provisions of the *Miranda* decision.

6. Material on the public and police controversy caused by the *Miranda* decision is developed from conversations with Kevin Mullen, Deputy Chief of Police (retired), San Francisco Police Department, and Maurice Lafferty; and personal knowledge of the authors. Additional information on the subject may be obtained from Paul D. Kamenar and Philip B. Heymann, "Pro and Con: The Miranda Decision—The Defendant's Rights vs. Police Efficiency," *New York Times*, Sunday, January 25, 1987. The article, employing a question-and-answer format, provides a balanced discussion, with Mr.

Kamenar representing the "pro" side of the argument, and Mr. Heymann the "con" side.

7. Germann, Day, and Gallati, *Introduction to Law Enforcement and Criminal Justice*, p. 103.
8. Material on the Edwin Meese suggestion concerning the alteration in the wording of the *Miranda* warning is developed from Jeffrey Toobin, "Viva Miranda," *The New Republic*, February 16, 1987, pp. 11–12; and Stephen Giller, "The Meese Lie," *The Nation*, February 21, 1987, p. 205.

CHAPTER FIVE

1. *Uniform Crime Reports for the United States* (Washington: Federal Bureau of Investigation, U.S. Department of Justice, 1986), p. 41.
2. *Uniform Crime Reports*, pp. 7, 16, 24.
3. Material on the news media and the television "cop" shows is developed from Samuel Walker, *The Police in America: An Introduction* (New York: McGraw-Hill, 1983), pp. 54–55.
4. Walker, pp. 54–59.
5. Walker, p. 207.
6. Material on the value of the patrolling cruiser is developed from conversations with Maurice Lafferty, Associate Professor, Administration of Justice Program, Marin Community College, Kentfield, Calif.
7. Material on police sources of information is developed from Charles E. Silberman, *Criminal Violence, Criminal Justice* (New York: Random House, 1978), pp. 225–227.
8. Additional and specific information on police investigations may be obtained from Thomas F. Adams, *Law Enforcement: An Introduction to the Police Role in the Community* (Englewood Cliffs, N.J.: Prentice-Hall, 1968), chapter 8, pp. 154–170.
9. Walker, pp. 140–142.
10. *Uniform Crime Reports*, p. 155.
11. Walker, pp. 53–54.
12. Silberman, *Criminal Violence, Criminal Justice*, p. 239.

CHAPTER SIX

1. Material on police bullying, harassment, and brutality is developed from Samuel Walker, *The Police in America: An Introduction* (New York: McGraw-Hill, 1983), pp. 206–208; Clemens Bartollas, Stuart J. Miller, and Paul B. Wice, *Participants in American Criminal*

Justice: The Promise and the Performance (Englewood Cliffs, N.J.: Prentice-Hall, 1983), pp. 120–121; Walter Arm, *The Policeman: An Inside Look at His Role in a Modern Society* (New York: Dutton, 1969), pp. 88–90. Additional information on the subject may be obtained from David Maraniss, "When the Law Turns Outlaw," *San Francisco Chronicle/Examiner*, October 5, 1986, reprint of an article in *Washington Post*.

2. Melinda Beck, with Martin Kasindorf, Anne Underwood, and Shawn Doherty, "New York's 'Bad Apples,' " *Newsweek*, May 6, 1985, p. 31.
3. Clarence Johnson, "Oakland Cops in Youth's Death Had Records of Violence," *San Francisco Chronicle*, September 24, 1986.
4. From a conversation with Maurice Lafferty, Associate Professor, Administration of Justice Program, Marin Community College, Kentfield, Calif.
5. From a conversation with a West Coast officer who asked not to be named.
6. Robert M. Fogelson, *Big-City Police* (Cambridge, Mass.: Harvard University Press, 1977), p. 240.
7. Fogelson, pp. 34, 240, 257–258.
8. From conversations with Maurice Lafferty and West Coast officers who asked not to be named.
9. From a conversation with a West Coast officer who asked not to be named.
10. From a conversation with the above officer.
11. From a conversation with a California policewoman who asked not to be named.
12. John G. Stratton, *Police Passages* (Manhattan Beach, Calif.: Glennon, 1984), p. 102.
13. James McClure, *Cop's World: Inside an American Police Force* (New York: Dell, 1984), pp. 94–95.
14. Louden Wainwright, "See No Evil, Hear No Evil, Be No Rat," *Life*, June, 1985, p. 7.
15. From conversations with West Coast officers who asked not to be named.
16. The material on Jerome Skolnick's views is derived from Walker, *The Police in America*, p. 206.
17. Walker, p. 206.
18. Material on police corruption is developed from: Herman Goldstein, *Policing a Free Society* (Cambridge, Mass.: Ballinger, 1977), pp. 93–94; Lawrence W. Sherman, "Becoming Bent: Moral Careers of Corrupt Policemen," an essay in *Police Corruption: A Sociological Perspective* (Garden City, NY.: Anchor, 1974), pp. 191–208; Walker, *The Police in America*. Additional information on the subject may be obtained from Richard J. Lundman, ed.,

Police Behavior: A Sociological Perspective (New York: Oxford University Press, 1980), chapter 5.

19. In Chapter Five, it was stated that officers often pay "snitches" money for information. Police do not consider this an unethical action. The use, however, of illegal goods for the purchase of information, while known to be a practice among some officers, is considered a corrupt act.
20. Bartollas, Miller, and Wice, *Participants in American Criminal Justice*, p. 117.
21. Wainright, "See No Evil, Hear No Evil, Be No Rat," p. 7.
22. Wainright, p. 7.
23. From a conversation with a West Coast officer who asked not to be named.

CHAPTER SEVEN

1. From a conversation with Maurice Lafferty, Associate Professor, Criminal Justice Program, Marin Community College, Kentfield, Calif.
2. Material on Internal Affairs is developed from George D. Eastman, ed., *Municipal Police Administration* (Washington: International City Management Association, 1969), pp. 203–207. Additional information on the subject may be obtained from Todd S. Purdum, "Every Police Bullet Fired Must Pass Many Layers of Inquiry," *New York Times*, January 25, 1987.
3. Clarence Johnson, "Oakland Police Call Shooting Self Defense," *San Francisco Chronicle*, September 26, 1986; and "Officer Faces No Charges in Oakland Killing," *San Francisco Chronicle*, October 16, 1986.
4. Melinda Beck, with Martin Kasindorf, Anne Underwood, and Shawn Doherty, "New York's 'Bad Apples,' " *Newsweek*, May 6, 1985, p. 31.
5. Personal knowledge of the authors.
6. Andrew C. Revkin, "Ordinary Dog, Extraordinary Sale," *San Francisco Chronicle*, December 27, 1986, reprint of an article in *Los Angeles Times*.
7. Material on the Newark program and the New York CPOP project is developed from Aric Press, "The Blues on Beat Street," *Newsweek*, January 28, 1985, p. 49; *Twenty-Five Year Report from the Vera Institute of Justice, 1961–1986* (New York: The Vera Institute of Justice, 1986), pp. 7–11.
8. A.C. Germann, Frank D. Day, and Robert R. J. Gallati, *Introduction to Law Enforcement and Criminal Justice*, rev. 6th printing (Springfield, Ill.: Charles C. Thomas, 1968), p. 257.

9. Material on the Chicago and Washington programs is developed from *The Challenge of Crime in a Free Society: A Report by the President's Commission on Law Enforcement and Administration of Justice* (Washington: United States Government Printing Office, 1967), p. 288.
10. Material on the San Diego CPOP program is developed from James McClure, *Cop World: Inside an American Police Force* (New York: Dell, 1984), pp. 19–26. Containing a great deal of information that provides insights not only into the San Diego Department but also into police work in general, the book is recommended to be read in its entirety.
11. Material on the pro and con opinions of the CPOP programs is developed from "Police Killings," *San Francisco Chronicle*, October 20, 1986; "The Blues on Beat Street," *Newsweek*, January 28, 1985, p. 49; conversations with Maurice Lafferty; and personal knowledge of the authors.
12. "The Blues on Beat Street," p. 49.

CHAPTER EIGHT

1. Material on the Civil Rights Act, the amendment of Title VII, and the affirmative action programs is developed from: Samuel Walker, *The Police in America: An Introduction* (New York: McGraw-Hill, 1983), pp. 262–264.
2. Material on the early history of women in police work is developed from Walter Arm, *The Policeman: An Inside Look at His Role in a Modern Society* (New York: Dutton, 1966), p. 22; Thomas F. Adams, *Law Enforcement: An Introduction to the Police Role in the Community* (Englewood Cliffs, N.J.: Prentice-Hall, 1936), pp. 37–39.
3. Material on the unrestricted duties of today's policewoman is developed from Ronald J. Waldron, *The Criminal Justice System: An Introduction*, 3d ed. (Boston: Houghton Mifflin, 1984), p. 189; conversations with Maurice Lafferty, Associate Professor, Administration of Justice Program, Marin Community College, Kentfield, Calif.
4. *Uniform Crime Reports for the United States* (Washington: Federal Bureau of Investigation, U.S. Department of Justice, 1986), p. 248.
5. Material on stories of policewomen being mistreated is developed from conversations with a California policewoman who prefers not to be named; Mary Ganz, "S.F. Cops: Women on the Way Up," *San Francisco Examiner*, October 27, 1986. Additional information on the problems of women in policing may be obtained from Mary

Ellen Abrecht with Barbara Lang Stern, *The Making of a Woman Cop* (New York: William Morrow, 1976); and Diane P. Muro, *Police Careers for Women* (New York: Julian Messner, 1979). Both books should be read in their entirety by young women interested in the topic or planning a career in law enforcement.

6. Ganz, "S.F. Cops: Women on the Way Up."
7. Conversation with Maurice Lafferty.
8. Waldron, *The Criminal Justice System*, p. 180.
9. Pamela D. Mayhall, *Police-Community Relations and the Administration of Justice* (New York: John Wiley, 1985), p. 120.
10. Mayhall, p. 115.
11. Mayhall, pp. 115–116.
12. *Statistical Abstract of the United States*, 1988 (Washington: U.S. Department of Commerce, Bureau of the Census, 1985), p. 403.
13. Miami Police Department; Walker, *The Police in America*, p. 261.
14. Material on researches into black officer–black community relations is developed from Mayhall, *Police-Community Relations and the Administration of Justice*, p. 117.
15. Material on the San Jose study is developed from Associated Press, "Black Cops Say Changes Needed," *San Francisco Chronicle*, January 11, 1987.
16. Walker, *The Police in America*, p. 263.
17. Waldron, pp. 177–178.

EPILOGUE

1. Material on the uses of technical gear in the future is developed from Tom Cook and James Metts, "A Police Officer's Day in 2001: A Futuristic Scenario," *The Futurist*, October 1985, p. 33; James R. Metts, "The Police Force of Tomorrow," *The Futurist*, October 1985, p. 31. Additional information on the topic may be obtained from Charles Bruno, "The Electronic Cops," *Datamation*, June 15, 1984, p. 115.
2. Material on the nature of police work in the future is derived from Metts, "The Police Force of Tomorrow," p. 31.

Recommended Reading

If you're interested in reading more about the American police and their work, you will find the following materials to be of both great interest and help.

BOOKS

Abrecht, Mary Ellen, with Stern, Barbara Lang. *The Making of a Woman Cop*. New York: William Morrow, 1976.

Adams, Thomas F. *Law Enforcement: An Introduction to the Police Role in the Community*. Englewood Cliffs, N.J.: Prentice-Hall, 1968.

—— *Police Field Operations*. Englewood Cliffs, N.J.: Prentice-Hall, 1985.

Arm, Walter. *The Policeman: An Inside Look at His Role in a Modern Society*. New York: Dutton, 1969.

Baker, Mark. *Cops: Their Lives in Their Own Words*. New York: Simon & Schuster, 1985.

Bartollas, Clemens; Miller, Stuart J.; and Wice, Paul B. *Participants in American Criminal Justice: The Promise and the Performance*. Englewood Cliffs, N.J.: Prentice-Hall, 1983.

Bayley, David H., and Mendelsohn, Harold. *Minorities and the Police: Confrontation in America*. New York: Free Press, 1969.

Eastman, George D., ed., and Eastman, Esther M., assoc. ed. *Municipal Police Administration*, 6th ed. Washington: International City Management Association, 1969.

Federal Bureau of Investigation, U.S. Department of Justice. *Uniform Crimes Reports for the United States*, 1985 ed. Washington: U.S. Department of Justice, 1986.

Fogelson, Robert M. *Big-City Police*. Cambridge, Mass.: Harvard University Press, 1977.

Garmire, Bernard L., ed. *Local Government Police Management*. Washington: International City Management Association, 1982.

Germann, A. C.; Day, Frank D.; and Gallati, Robert R. *Introduction to Law Enforcement and Criminal Justice*, rev. 6th printing. Springfield, Ill.: Charles C. Thomas, 1968.

Lundman, Richard J., ed. *Police Behavior: A Sociological Perspective*. New York: Oxford University Press, 1980.

Manning, Peter K. Police Work. Cambridge, Mass.: The M.I.T. Press, 1977.

Mayhall, Pamela D. *Police-Community Relations and the Administration of Justice*, 3d ed. New York: John Wiley, 1985.

McClure, James. *Cop World: Inside an American Police Force*. New York: Dell, 1986.

Muro, Diane P. *Police Careers for Women*. New York: Julian Messner, 1979.

Neier, Aryeh. *Defending My Enemy*. New York: Dutton, 1979.

Pantell, Dora, and Greenidge, Edwin. *If Not Now, When?* New York: Delacorte, 1969.

The President's Commission on Law Enforcement and Administration of Justice. *The Challenge of Crime in a Free Society*. Washington: United States Government Printing Office, 1967.

Reiss, Albert. *The Police and the Public*. New Haven, Conn.: Yale University Press, 1971.

Silberman, Charles E. *Criminal Violence, Criminal Justice*. New York: Random House, 1978.

Skolnick, Jerome. *The Police and the Urban Ghetto*. Chicago: American Bar Foundation, 1968.

Smith, Ralph Lee. *The Tarnished Badge*. New York: Thomas Y. Crowell, 1965.

Stratton, John G. *Police Passages*. Manhattan Beach, Calif.: Glennon, 1984.

Stuckey, Gilbert B. *Procedures in the Justice System*, 2d ed. Columbus, Ohio: Charles E. Merrill, 1980.

Torbet, Floyd James. *Policemen the World Over*. New York: Hastings House, 1965.

Waldron, Robert J. *The Criminal Justice System: An Introduction*, 3d ed. Boston: Houghton Mifflin, 1984.

168

Walker, Samuel. *The Police in America: An Introduction*. New York: McGraw-Hill, 1983.

Wilson, O. W., and McLaren, Roy C. Police Administration, 4th ed. New York: McGraw-Hill, 1977.

MAGAZINE AND NEWSPAPER ARTICLES

Ammann, Edward P., and Hey, Jim. "Establishing Agency Personnel Levels." *FBI Law Enforcement Bulletin*, July 1986.

Aric Press. "The Blues on Blue Street." *Newsweek*, January 28, 1985.

Beck, Melinda; with Kasindorf, Martin; Underwood, Anne; and Doherty, Shawn. "New York's Bad Apples." *Newsweek*, May 6, 1985.

Bruno, Charles. "The Electronic Cops." *Datamation*, June 15, 1984.

Cook, Tom, and Metts, James. "A Police Officer's Day in 2001: A Futuristic Scenario. *The Futurist*, October 1985.

"High-Tech Big Brother." *Scientific American*, January 1986.

Inbau, Fred E. "Over-Reaction—The Mischief of Miranda v. Arizona. *FBI Law Enforcement Bulletin*, April 1983.

Kamenar, Paul D. and Heymann, Philip B. "Pro and Con: The Miranda Ruling. The Defendant's Rights vs. Police Efficiency." *New York Times*, January 25, 1987.

Maraniss, David. "When the Law Turns Outlaw." *San Francisco Chronicle-Examiner*, October 6, 1986 (reprinted from *Washington Post*).

Metts, James R. "The Police Force of Tomorrow." *The Futurist*, October 1985.

Purdum, Todd S. "Every Police Bullet Must Pass Many Layers of Inquiry." *New York Times*, January 25, 1987.

Wainwright, Louden. "See No Evil, Hear No Evil, Be No Rat." *Life*, June 1985.

Index

About The Authors

Edward F. Dolan, a native Californian, has written more than seventy nonfiction books for young people and adults. Margaret M. Scariano, who was born in Montana, is the author of eighteen novels and three nonfiction books for young people and adults. This book is the second they have written together. Their first was *Cuba and the United States: Troubled Neighbors*, published by Franklin Watts. Their homes are in northern California, near San Francisco.